# From Armoured Cars to Coldstream Guards

DILLWYN PARRISH STARR

CAPTAIN GROTON FOOTBALL ELEVEN

# From Armoured Cars to Coldstream Guards

An American Volunteer During the First
World War

ILLUSTRATED

Louis Starr

The Battle of the Somme, 1916: Third Stage
John Buchan

**LEONAUR**

*From Armoured Cars to Coldstream Guards*
*An American Volunteer During the First World War*
by Louis Starr
*The Battle of the Somme, 1916: Third Stage*
by John Buchan

ILLUSTRATED

FIRST EDITION

Leonaur is an imprint of Oakpast Ltd
Copyright in this form © 2023 Oakpast Ltd

ISBN: 978-1-916535-20-6 (hardcover)
ISBN: 978-1-916535-21-3 (softcover)

**http://www.leonaur.com**

Publisher's Notes

# Contents

To

His Many Friends in Recognition of the
Joy They Brought Him in Life and
Of Their Abiding Love
And Loyalty

# Foreword

Apart from my affection for my son I have been impelled to compile this short memoir by my pride in his very gallant record, and by a desire to tell his friends, whom I believe to be interested, the details of his two years' war service.

A soldier comrade of his writes me, on learning that the manuscript is finished: "May I read it? I knew that he kept a diary and know some of his experiences, though there are some parts that I do not know. And as a record of good work finely done your book will be worth reading." To make it worth reading and make it worthy of him has been my rather ambitious purpose. I can only approximately accomplish this. But I shall have given him my homage and shall have done for him all that is left for me to do since he has gone "over the top," never to return.

Louis Starr.

123, Pall Mall,
London, 1917.

# The War Story of Dillwyn Parrish Starr

1

Dillwyn's Groton and Harvard days, when his football achievements kept him much in evidence, are even better known to his friends than to me. To this part of his life, therefore, I shall not refer, but pass at once to the two years preceding his very gallant ending and tell how he fulfilled his early promise of conspicuous courage, and kept the lovable sweetness of disposition, we all knew, through the hardships and annoying petty trials of active service, both as an orderly with the ambulance corps and as a soldier in the field. The intimate details and his impressions are taken from his letters and his diary, which he kept with great regularity while on duty.

The outbreak of the great European war on August 4th, 1914, found Dillwyn at Islesboro, Maine, toward the end of a summer holiday. He was interested at once, and we talked of the invasion of Belgium and discussed whether the United States could honourably remain neutral, or was in duty bound to interfere on the side of the Allies. He did not at first realise that American ideals demanded and American safety required the overthrow of grasping German tyranny. A state of mind quite natural considering our isolation from the struggle. For the war seemed very distant, if not almost unbelievable, in this island colony where all is very peaceful, with little change from year to year, and where his thoughts were tempted to the out-door sports he so thoroughly enjoyed.

Still, a fuller appreciation soon began to dawn. Going to New York late in August he came in closer touch with, and heard more about foreign affairs, and on Labour Day, while lying on the sands at Long Beach reading the war reports, he suddenly told the friends who were with him that he had determined "to see the war."

With this object he went to the office of his friend Elliot Bacon to offer his services to the "American Ambulance "in which his father,

11

S.S. HAMBURG, HOSPITAL SHIP

Robert Bacon, was interested. There he happened to meet George Ball who told him of a position which had been offered him on the S.S. *Hamburg*, recently fitted out as a Red Cross ship, but as he was unable to accept it, he would ask to have it transferred. This Dillwyn accepted, and soon received the appointment.

The *Hamburg*, repainted white with a huge red cross on either side, was bound for France with a corps of doctors and nurses and a complement of medical supplies. After many postponements she left New York on September 13th for a memorable voyage. First, she was delayed several days at Sandy Hook to discharge her German crew which had been replaced by a make-shift lot of white and black substitutes.

After she really got off, the latter were found to be entirely untrained hands, and besides soon began a racial contest which from time to time broke into actual combats. The Germans, also, before departing had tampered with the ship's machinery and thrown overboard many necessary tools; so altogether it became a question whether port could ever be reached. Under these conditions, the voyage must have been most uncomfortable, but Dillwyn writes of it:

> I was one of the crew. At first, I slept in a cabin with two pretty strange men, and ate with the roughest you ever saw. The food was awful. However, I made friends with Mr. Delaney, the chief engineer, and after a few days he gave me a cabin to myself and I had the freedom of the ship. Some of the doctors were fine, and when there was nothing doing, we got up poker games.

The *Hamburg* called at Falmouth on September 24th, and Dillwyn left her with the full acquiescence of Delaney and with a written certificate as to ability and character from him.

From Falmouth he went directly to London, and a few days later met Walter Oakman, and, through him, Richard Norton, who was recruiting and collecting cars for his "American Volunteer Motor Ambulance Corps."

**★★★★★★★★★★**

Walter G. Oakman, Junr., Harvard '07, has since been very closely associated with Dillwyn. He was with him in the Ambulance Corps and in Flanders with the Armoured Cars, and they were both promoted at the same time. Shortly after receiving his commission in the R.N.V.R., he was ordered back to Flanders during the German effort to reach Calais. Later, he joined the Guards, preceded him to France and returned severely wounded before Dillwyn had finished his train-

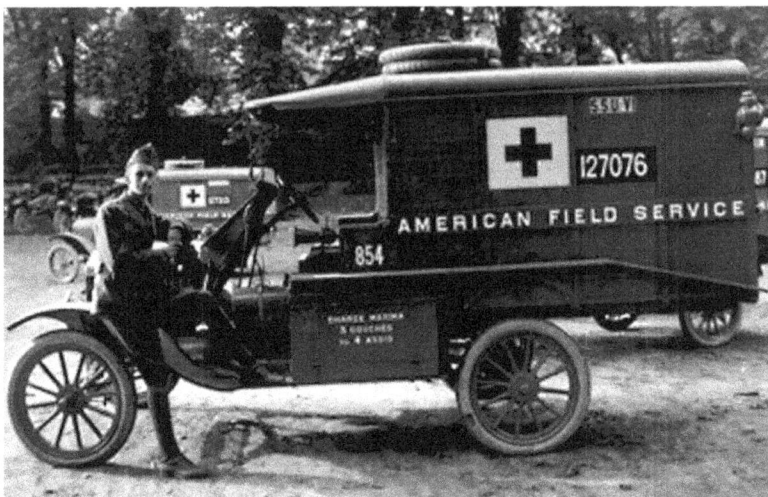

AMERICAN VOLUNTEER AMBULANCE

AMERICAN VOLUNTEER AMBULANCE IN ACTION WITH THE FRENCH ARMY

ing at Windsor. He was a most steadfast friend and a thorough soldier, and won Dillwyn's admiration by his great bravery.

★★★★★★★★★★

His offer of service met with ready acceptance for a position combining ambulance driver and orderly, requiring, in addition to the ordinary qualifications of a chauffeur some knowledge of "first aid," and the proper methods of handling the wounded. With such training and the getting together of his outfit he was engaged until October 19th—little more than a month after sailing from home—when he left London for the object of his desire—France and the front. The car in which he ran to Folkestone and shipped for Boulogne was a gift from Alan Loney to the corps.

★★★★★★★★★★

Loney subsequently lost his life when the *Lusitania* was torpedoed. His death was deeply regretted, as his work with the wounded was excellent and his generosity in gifts of ambulance cars beyond praise, as were also his successful efforts in cultivating a like liberality in others.

★★★★★★★★★

It was a powerful Mercedes fitted with a large ambulance body, and, on reaching France, was transferred with its crew to the British Red Cross, which was in need of a large ambulance to make up a unit. In consequence Dillwyn, with his usual good fortune, began to see service without the delay which fell to the lot of the other cars making up the bulk of Norton's corps.

During the first week he was kept on duty at Boulogne, every day and sometimes late into the night, carrying to hospitals the wounded arriving by railway train from the battlefields near Arras, and Lille. These men brought various wonderful yarns. For example, he quotes in his notes;

They tell us fighting the worst of the war; Allies outnumbered ten to one; German artillery fine, but rifle fire no good, our men killing three to one.

Also, "war will be over by Christmas," and "Indian troops carry German heads as souvenirs."

His diary may now take up the account of his daily work.

*October 27th, 1914.* "Lined up at 9 a.m. for call to St. Omer. Started at 1.30 p.m., arrived at 4.30, having stopped several times on way. Saw transports, aeroplanes, and English cavalry. Met other ambulances at Cattlemarket. Now under strict orders, many sleeping in cars."

*October 28th.* "Up at 7 a.m. Orders to leave at 2 p.m. Watched target practice and walked through park and cathedral, which is very old with quaint statues, some of thirteenth century; people at prayers all dressed in black. Left St. Omer at 3 p.m., arrived Bailleul at 6 o'clock. Were put up at French house and given tea before going to bed; family, refugees from Lille with nine children, refused payment for accommodation. Germans had been in same house on October 10th; reported to have behaved well."

*October 29th.* "Walked about town and met wounded Indians walking from one hospital to another. In afternoon took squad of Indians to railway station; no officials about, so managed them myself. Heard heavy gun-firing during day and one bomb dropped by station—no damage."

*October 30th.* "Up at 6 a.m., breakfast in car in front of station. At 9 got off and ran to Armentieres. Guns, a quarter of a mile away, firing at rate of thirty times a minute. Saw aeroplanes being bombarded by Germans; could see smoke puffs of bursting shells apparently a mile in air but wide of mark. Moved 'sitting-up' cases. After lunch, worked at car. Ready to start at 2 o'clock, but waited about until 6 and then started for Nieppe and 'Plug Street' (Ploegsteert). Took badge off arm, put lights out, and got within seventy yards of firing line with guns behind; battlefield a level plain. Heard that our line was too thin and not enough English artillery. Germans outnumbering British had broken through one sector. Took back 'sitting-up' cases to Bailleul, arriving at midnight."

*October 31st.* "Many French troops passing through town. Firing at aeroplane frightens Indian wounded, who think hospital is being bombarded. Rumours of Germans entering Nieppe and town being evacuated. Heavy firing all day; enemy advance. Cleared hospital."

*November 1st.* "Left at 9 a.m. for Neuve Eglise, being near line and enemy advancing, our men retreating. Wounded—first bad cases—brought from field by horse-vans and we took them to hospital. Later, ordered to Locre. Saw cavalry on road and at dusk, just as we were rounding a bend, a shell burst fifty or sixty yards in front of us—two gunners and four horses killed. Germans, having range, another shell burst near us and troops began to retire. Picked up wounded at small village nearby and started for home (Bailleul). Passed thousands of French infantry and English cavalry and artillery—all cheerful—probably an army corps in all. Were checked often by blocks, and by our wounded begging us to stop or to go slowly."

For the next fortnight the diary shows, as he tersely puts it, "nothing doing." There seems to have been an interruption of work, perhaps because there was little fighting going on, and he motored back to Boulogne, then to Doullens—rejoining Norton's corps—and finally to Paris. There he found everything "shut up, no street lamps lighted at night, but searchlights playing." When not on the road he passed the time walking in the country, looking about any little town he happened to be in and visiting neighbouring hospitals and cathedrals. He was back in Doullens on the 14th, eager for work, but had no calls. Of this day, he writes, "Walked in morning; after lunch went to a coursing meet," and of the next:

Walked in morning, explored a cave in afternoon. Saw Ned Toland who is working at the Harjes Hospital near Montdidier. He says some of the wounds are awful.

Then follow three more days of idleness. On one of these he motored to the east of Doullens:

Many troops about quaint villages, saw trenches and dug-outs, latter had sleeping shelves about two feet from floor, straw for bedding. Some had water covering floor. Men in these trenches, French; all seemed very cold; gave my gloves to one. While here our big guns began firing a hundred yards in front of us and German guns from a wood to the North.

On another day:

Ran towards Arras, see German shells falling in field to right. Entered Beaumetz and gave soldiers cigarettes. Heavy cannonading. Stopped by officer as we were out of our army division and password 'Arras' didn't go, but got through and directly behind French artillery, guns also firing overhead on right. French troops entrenched along road. Went six kilometres towards Arras from Beaumetz before turning back and met three thousand or more Arab cavalry coming over hill on white ponies, prancing and full of life. Men were dressed in varied colours, some with bright red cloaks; they formed in fours as they came to the road, right upon us, and rode to the north. Arrived Doullens at dusk.

17

*November 19th.* "Carried wounded from citadel to railway station."

This was followed by another interval—five days—of "killing time," the only note worth mentioning being a visit to a:

French hospital; no heating. Wounded lying on straw in awful cold.

*November 24th.* "Cleared wounded to railway station, moving forty-seven 'sitting-up' cases in all, carried one man on back about a hundred yards up track."

*November 25th.* "Moved ten wounded to station. Ordered to go to Albert and arrived 3.30 p.m. All houses near church down and many burnt. Absolute ruin for blocks; people looking very poor and starved. Saw Germans shelling French aeroplane. Home (Doullens) at 5 o'clock. Captain Moore-Brabazon here, reports it quiet all along the front. Moore-Brabazon is in Royal Flying Corps and offers to try to get Oakman and me into the Armoured Motor Car Division."

This promise was so promptly fulfilled that in ten days a letter arrived with instructions to apply for enlistment. In the meantime, Dillwyn with a single ambulance was transferred to Montdidier and did rather more work with the wounded. The only matter of interest he records is that after going to Duvy for monthly passports:

Got lost on way back and nearly went into the German lines.

On the receipt of the welcome letter, December 5th, he and Oakman immediately began preparations for leaving France. On the 9th he picked Oakman up at Compiegne and ran back through Montdidier to Doullens, where they saw their chief and obtained their release. Next day they started for Boulogne, arrived at 10 a.m. and caught the boat just in time. Reaching London early in the afternoon they went directly to Wormwood Scrubbs, the depot of the Armoured Cars and made application for enlistment. They were accepted and ordered to report for duty at 10 o'clock on the following morning. Thus ends his connection with Norton's corps.

Though always enthusiastic about any project that promised activity, I think he never particularly fancied ambulance work. I know that from the very first he disliked the idea of being protected by a red cross on his sleeve, while so many about him were enlisted to do soldiers' work. Still, he regretted leaving Richard Norton. He had seen the corps' steady development under its able founder and realised the importance and growing scope of its beneficent work. Further, his short two months' experience with the wounded had shown him that the German methods of making war were so brutal and foul that he came to long, as he said later, "to get at them with cold steel." And the conviction grew strong within him that the place for a free man was on the side of the Allies fighting for liberty, justice, civilization—the world's cause; and he began to feel, too, the importance of the issue to his own country. Consequently, he eagerly embraced the first opportunity to enlist.

2

The Armoured Motor Car Division attached, strangely enough, to the Royal Naval Air Service, comprised 23 squadrons of 15 cars each; 12 light and 3 heavy. The light cars were of Rolls Royce and Lanchester makes, having about 40-horsepower engines and with somewhat boat-shaped bodies, sharp in front and broad behind, and protected by 3/8-inch armour plates. The light cars carried a Maxim gun and three men; the heavy—really 9-ton trucks or lorries—with square armoured bodies and American chassis, mounted one 3-pound gun, and carried six men, and it was to the crew of one of these that Dillwyn was ultimately detailed.

The rank and file of the division, one of which he became by enlistment, was composed of men presumed to be more or less expert mechanicians, manually more skilled and capable than the ordinary recruit, and all held the rank of Petty Officers, a status somewhat above the lowest, though of little moment as far as discipline and duties were concerned. Most of his companions were professional chauffeurs or working engineers. He found them "good fellows" and liked their rough but hearty friendship.

Such were the conditions under which he been training on December 12th. He had to be out of bed by 6.30 in the morning and was on duty from 8 o'clock until 5 in the afternoon. These nine hours, with an interval for the mid-day meal, were occupied in squad-drilling in formations and with arms, as each man carried a rifle and bayonet; in range shooting; route marching; manoeuvring with the light and heavier cars; Maxim drill with practice in taking apart and reassembling these guns; semaphore practice; lectures on practical military subjects, and various odds and ends, such as unpacking and cleaning motor-cars and clearing up garages and yards.

At one time he was detailed as P.O. (Petty Officer) in charge to

LANCHESTER ARMOURED TRANSPORT

take eleven men to Southwold, Suffolk, where they remained two weeks, in billets, three or four men sleeping in one small room, and with days passed in route marching and shooting on a range with Maxim and rifle. All day long he was in the open air and exercising, and, as he writes, "got full of health." Later he was sent with a squad to the Talbot factories where they both worked on motorcars and mounted guard.

So, the time passed busily until March 1st, 1915, when he left London with Squadron No. 2 for the front. This squadron, commanded by the Duke of Westminster, was composed of twelve light and three heavy cars, several supply cars and twenty-four motorcycles intended for dispatch work. Every car was designated by some name, Dillwyn's being called the "Black Joke." The personnel was eight officers and 120 men.

At Wormwood Scrubbs there is a long lane running from the Headquarters buildings to the high-road. Down this lane we saw them start on their journey. Advancing towards us in single file and accurately spaced, with the men in their smart navy-blue uniforms, with the navy flag flying from a staff in the front of each steel-clad car and with the wicked-looking muzzles of the guns just showing, it was a most inspiring spectacle, bringing to mind one's idea of old-time knights in armour going into battle. They came swiftly, wheeled to the right on reaching the road, and in a few moments were well on their way and lost to sight.

The first stop was Cowden, Kent. Here they went into billets, had target-practice with Maxim gun and 3-pounder, and were inspected by the duke. At 10.30 a.m. on the 5th, the whole squad started for Dover, but Dillwyn's 3-pounder lorry met with a mishap, was much delayed in the righting, and did not arrive until 2 a.m. on the following morning, having to make most of the run during the night, which was "beautifully moon-light." By 2 o'clock on the same day, March 6th, the heavy cars were loaded on a transport. She sailed at 5 p.m., had a smooth trip, reached the dock at Dunkirk at 5 a.m. next day, and by 7 o'clock all were disembarked.

Through the kindness of the First Sea Lord, Admiral Lord Fisher, his mother and I were on the pier at Dover to see the departure. The transport was small and a mere unpainted shell of a vessel. She had no upper deck, being quite open to the sky above the main deck, on which the tarpaulin-covered cars stood, and was entirely without shelter or accommodation for passengers. However, the men accepted what we thought their hard lot without complaint, and when their ship cast off, sang and cheered in the delight of at last being on the way to the real thing. To us, the sight of the ugly vessel slowly blundering away and disappearing in the gathering darkness was very depressing. Taking up the diary again:

*March 7th.* "Went to St. Pol, and on this day and the 8th and 9th were on guard duty and slept all night on the floor of a dancehall."

*March 10th.* "Orders to go to the front immediately. Get ammunition, board car, and leave at 3 p.m. for Merville. Passed through St. Omer, where I bought three slices of bread for a shilling; then through Aire, and reach Merville at 11 p.m. Find town the headquarters of British. Big battle going on, and many wounded coming in."

*March 11th.* "Best day so far. Up at 4.30 a.m.; had coffee, and after mending car, which had bad brake trouble, started for Armentieres. Taking wrong road, at first, had to turn back and try again. At Armentieres met many soldiers who wished us luck and told us to 'give it to them.' Our job was to shoot up a barn occupied by Germans near Laventie. Arrived at Laventie about 11 o'clock, ran car along narrow road, passing many batteries, and stopped near a corner where guns roared all about us. Ten minutes later German shell struck and burst in the road twenty yards away throwing stones and dirt over car, and after a few minutes another broke further away, and still another, knocking down two men.

We could hear them coming through the air and tell by their whistle whether they were going over us or were about to strike near. Too foggy to find range of our barn, so returned to Laventie. After lunch advanced again, the duke coming in our car, and passed over spot where first shell struck and made a hole in road over three feet deep. It had been filled with stones, but we sank in about a foot. Went further along road, with an English officer guiding, and under rifle fire, had action. First shot going just over target, others striking. Returned safely to Laventie though exposed to shrapnel fire; saw big shells bursting, but not very near. Through it all the behaviour of men fine. After securing billets visited Armoured Train and met gunners, who took me aboard. When they fired 4.7 and 6-inch guns, discharges rocked the whole car."

*March 12th.* "Out of bed at 6.30 a.m., hear shells whistling over our quarters and many bursting in town, four people killed. The duke

On the way overseas

came at 10 o'clock and called us out. Went to same place as yesterday. German artillery trying to find batteries behind us and shells were dropping fast, could hear shells from our own 1 5-inch guns passing overhead. Went into action, firing twenty-three rounds, shelling a small village, and enabling our infantry to occupy it thirty minutes afterwards. In afternoon took up another position, being ditched on the way owing to hurry, and fired eighty-two shells. Big action going on with incendiary bombs and many shells. Barn and house burning near. Getting out of ditch were followed by bursting shrapnel."

*March 13th.* "Hot day! Up at 3 a.m. and on guard. Shells still passing over and falling in town. The duke came at 9 o'clock to take us out. Went in same direction as yesterday afternoon but to more advanced post. Heavy fighting going on. Took up position 200 yards south of cross-roads at Fauquissart, behind some buildings which were half battered down. Got range of house occupied by Germans who were holding up our advance and fired forty-two shells all telling and driving them out. They were shot down by our infantry, who occupied what was left of the building a short time afterward.

"Enemy artillery found us, and their shells began dropping all about us; also under rifle fire, and had to keep cover. Shells were striking ten yards away in the mud and one splashed water into the car. Finally obliged to back away, as road too cramped to turn; moved very slowly and it seemed we were going to get it sure—close squeeze! Got back to Laventie at 11 o'clock and in afternoon (striking contrast) painted car and had my hair cut."

The Armoured Car actions of these three days were a part of the battle of Neuve Chapelle, the object of which the diary suggests "was to straighten out the Allies' line between Armentieres and La Bassée," and "it was reported that eight thousand men had been killed in the action on a front of six miles."

*March 14th.* "Laventie subjected to bombardment. Firing, at first, seemed distant. Soon drew near and bombs began bursting in street. Went into house that was struck; found people inside quite unconscious of it; the shell had only knocked out some bricks at the top and scattered shrapnel bullets over the upper floor. Women of town ran about seeking shelter in cellars."

The following day the "Black Joke" was relieved and went with its crew back to Dunkirk for a rest. Dillwyn makes a circumstance of getting half a day off, and the remainder of the time was occupied in guard duty, in cleaning and tuning up the car, looking after its armour plating and in manoeuvres. He took, with the other petty officers, his turn at cooking, slept where he could find a roof to cover him, often on a bare floor or in a hay loft; notes the fact that once he was fortunate enough to be able to steal some straw for bedding, and on the 24th that he "slept in a bed for the first time in eighteen days."

Again, he tells of the luxury of having a bath in a tub, though taken practically in public and in company with a number of other men. Making little account of the work, hardship and bad weather, he writes more fully of the beauty of moon-lit nights, of wonderful days and glorious rainbows and sunsets.

By March 24th he was again near the front in Armentieres and experienced another trifling and unexpected bombardment of which he says:

Strange sensation when everything quiet, and all of a sudden hear the sound of a coming bomb and then an explosion.

On the 25th there was a parade of the armoured cars, reviewed by the general, who found everything quite satisfactory. Also, the word was passed that they were going into action very soon. The idea being as follows:

Take up position on Lille road about one hundred yards behind own trenches. Light cars carrying Maxim guns to sweep the enemy's trenches about two hundred yards away. Heavier car with the 3-pounder to batter down, at longer range, a house occupied by snipers.

*March 27th.* "Roused at 6.30 a.m. by woman coming into our sleeping-shed with coffee while we were still wrapped in our blankets. Beautiful day. Had practice with cars. Many aeroplanes about, one German machine came over us but was driven back by one shot. Much firing of anti-aircraft guns during morning and could see dozens of shells bursting; in the air. In afternoon were told to get some sleep and I did, sitting in chair. At 4 o'clock had tea.

"Thinking of going out gives me the same feeling as before a football match. Start at 7.30 p.m. in beautiful moonlight, go slowly along road toward Lille and after half an hour's run come to Chapelle d'Armentières and a cross road. Go down this and leave car and clear away trees, helped by Tommies and Hussars. Walk further down road with Officer Commanding and Oakman, where we were to take up position later, about two hundred and fifty yards from German trenches. Hear shots from snipers and a few bullets whistle overhead, otherwise very quiet. Saw a number of star shells and could clearly see trenches. Came back to car and tried to sleep; later got some coffee and a little sleep in a roundhouse."

*March 28th.* "Off at 4 a.m., in beautiful morning, for selected spot. Took position and began action, firing forty-two shots at snipers' house with little reply, though we expected a lot; Maxims keeping the enemy in their trenches. Think we withdrew too quickly, our O.C. becoming excited. Would have done more had we stayed longer. Went back to Chapelle d'Armentières for breakfast and I looked over a ruined church I saw in the moonlight last night. Rested remainder of day."

On March 29th, he took part in a small action from a hamlet near Chapelle d'Armentières, his gun firing seventeen shots. He was in another action on April 2nd. For this he started from Armentières to take up position at 10 o'clock in the evening, reached the firing line in an hour and walked along a communicating trench to get a clearer view of a house which was to be the target. Afterward the whole crew, including the duke, sat up in their car until 4.30 a.m.

Rifle bullets were buzzing about. Some struck very near. The duke said he couldn't understand us coming so far for this. Began action at 3 o'clock and fired twenty-eight rounds. Could have done much more had we kept up longer, but we were ordered to cease firing.

Next day they were relieved and returned to Dunkirk.

Then followed a little more than a month of routine fatigue duty. He "returned to Laventie," where he "found church had been practically destroyed since we were last here, many Jack Johnsons having knocked down tower and neighbouring houses; village practically deserted," and with the car moved about from place to place, near Armentières, Merville, Aubers, Fleurbaix and Bailleul.

During this interval his diary shows that he had more time to himself. He occupied much of this leisure in walking among the trenches, and getting as close to the firing line as possible, often being in areas of German gunfire. In this way he must have improved, greatly, his general knowledge of the fighting and of the battle ground about Aubers,

Neuve Chapelle and la Bassée. Several times a village, where he happened to be billeted, came under bombardment without much harm being done, and the experience became common enough to elicit no more comment than a passing mention.

*May 6th.* "In Laventie. We are going into action from the same road we took for attack near Fauquissart. In the evening, carry ammunition to firing place. Rifle bullets whizzing about."

On May 7th the order was cancelled, but on the 8th:

At 9 p.m. started for line, reached first houses of Fauquissart and backed up car on right side of road. With poles we cut from trees, carried two boxes of ammunition farther along road and hid them behind a ruined house; also moved shells we had brought yesterday. Rifle bullets striking fast and many star shells showing. Plan of general attack was for Indians to march from right, and 8th Corps from left and advance to Aubers, and 7th Corps assisting, drive Germans back and enter Lille early in afternoon; 50,000 casualties expected. Slept in car.

*May 9th.* "Up at 2 a.m. Started for firing front but car was driven too near edge of road and slid into deep ditch. Every one disgusted with prospect of missing the most important engagement we've had. Took gun and ammunition off car and hid them in cellar of partly ruined house, where we later found shelter. I went up to the top story and saw everything. Our guns started at 5 o'clock. The bombardment was tremendous and I could see the shells dropping in the German trenches and the shrapnel bursting over them. The Germans soon began to reply. Their shells seemed to be mostly directed towards Aubers, but a few struck in front of us, and later they sent over about twenty 6-inch shells which hit house and fell in road.

"Car surrounded by shells, but not touched except by small splinter which hardly marked it. By 10 a.m. fire slackened and we began righting car. Finished by 5 o'clock in afternoon, and we replaced gun and ammunition. During the evening, enemy's bombardment was renewed and there was considerable Maxim firing. Tried to sleep, but at midnight were recalled and reached Laventie at 2 a.m. The whole action was given up as German positions were too strong, very heavily manned and too costly to take. Our crew praised for righting and bringing back car, gun, and ammunition."

There is one page of the diary which should be quoted here as it illustrates so well his real sweetness of disposition, and his uniform inclination to be just and avoid controversies. Evidently after some slight disagreement with one of his fellows he inserts what he thinks of him and then:

I suppose I'm a chump for writing this, but it relieves my mind.

A few days later he writes:

Here and now I take back all I said of ————. I have been with him under fire and he was as cool as a cucumber. But I will leave it in just to show what a goat I am.

To go back to the story:

*May 10th.* "Got up late and changed clothes in field. At noon the duke came and told Oakman and me that we had been promoted and were to report in London on the 14th."

On the next day they were sent with car and crew to Béthune. Here, living under canvas, they were kept—another battle being expected—until May 15th, when they were relieved, and immediately set out for England *via* Dunkirk, and arrived at mid-day on the 17th.

We were taken by surprise when he walked into our apartment in London and announced that he was to be promoted. He seemed rather service worn, but looked hard and fit and happy. As was his way, he said little about his exploits and nothing of his hardships and trials. His conversation was about his liking for active campaigning and of the splendid courage and cheerfulness of the British soldier.

The Germans he thoroughly despised for their barbarous methods, though recognising their organising and fighting qualities, and he spoke of their strength, in men and position, on the western front, expressing his belief that neither army would ever be able really to break the line of the other.

His stay with us was very brief. In ten days, he had received his promotion and was gazetted Sub-Lieutenant, Royal Navy Volunteer Reserves, a navy rank corresponding with full lieutenant in the army, and had accepted an offer for duty in Gallipoli, where there were already two Armoured Car Squadrons. This latter he hailed with great eagerness, as promising unusual opportunities for active service. In the meantime, he had procured his officer's uniform (khaki now) and renewed his kit, and on May 28th was on his way to Hythe, to join a detachment of Armoured Car men who were there, in reserve, taking

DILLWYN PARRISH STARR
ROYAL NAVY VOLUNTEER RESERVE
ARMOURED CAR DIVISION

Maxim training.

His mother and I took a party to spend the week-end with him on June 5th at Hythe, a quiet out-of-the-way place near Folkestone. His fellow officers were not over congenial, and his duties occupied only a few of the early morning hours, so there was nothing to do the rest of the day. He carried a Maxim gun lock in his pocket which he took apart and put together from time to time, and a little book on gunnery which he studied. Both in preparation for a proposed examination, which, by the way, never came off.

He was possessed by the idea that months would pass before he would be called to active duty, as his C.O. was a firm believer in thorough training, and thought no time wasted in obtaining it. His restlessness, however, was soon to be relieved, for on the next day an order came to report at headquarters, and early on the morning of the 7th he, with another officer, and a draft of twenty-five men, entrained for London, and on the same night, for Plymouth, where they took transport for Gallipoli.

The following letter to his cousin, Gladys Parrish, deals with his departure:

Plymouth, June 9th, 1915.

After I took you home last night I went to Paddington and the train had left sooner than expected. I got hold of the Station Master and the Military Authorities, and was allowed to go on the newspaper train which made no stops and got in fifty minutes after the other, which started three hours before. The boat is comfortable and full of troops and mules, etc. I expect it will be great fun on the sea again, and the trip will pass only too quickly. The boat is called *The Manitou* and has been torpedoed once but patched up again.

Your pipe is a corker, and the cigarettes and tobacco great. I shall remember you when I smoke and the good times we have had together. Norman Armour, whom I met by chance on Monday, sent me a camera and films, which I have found in my bag. It was mighty nice of him.

As far as I can gather from all I hear here, the War Office and the Admiralty are all up in the air. Things at the Dardanelles are not very good, and we have only advanced three miles. I believe the War Office and the Admiralty are at odds, and that they are going to take over our corps into the army. Why these men

30

MAXIM GUN AT GALLIPOLI

can't all get together in a time like this beats me.

We start this afternoon, so lots of love to you and the family.

## 3

The world realises now that the Dardanelles expedition was a ghastly blunder, which led to the political death of a prominent minister, and the ruin of the military reputation of a supposedly great general; besides being attended by the suffering and useless slaughter of thousands of the very bravest men.

★★★★★★★★★★

Amongst them a friend, Colonel H. J. Johnston, D.S.O., was wounded in both legs in the attack after the Suvla landing. His men tried to bring him back, but he refused to allow them, saying: "No, leave me, take the boys first," and the Turks advancing, he has not been heard of since.

★★★★★★★★★★

Originally a brilliant conception, it failed because its poor and hasty planning was still more indifferently executed. If a sufficient, combined land and sea, force had been despatched at first, the troops might have landed without opposition and have paraded to Constantinople, while the warships engaged the only defences there were—those on the Eastern coast—so say the experts. But a gambler's chance was taken with the fleet and disastrously failed.

Next, came delay in transporting soldiers, and the Turks warned of coming trouble had time, under their German drivers, thoroughly to fortify all of the commanding positions on the Peninsula. Then came inconceivable muddling with the army. How deep this was may be imagined when we know that the campaign was directed mainly from a distant island and without even proper maps of the ground over which the troops were engaged.

The mismanagement and lack of organization and forethought are indicated throughout Dillwyn's daily records, which were resumed as soon as he was fairly off, and also in his letters, written chiefly to his mother, with whom he corresponded with great affection and regularity. These continue the story:

*June 9th.* "Wrote the family this morning. Our transport left Plymouth at 7.10 p.m. attended by two torpedo boats, and all lights were put out when we reached the open sea."

The voyage was slow and uneventful. On the 14th they touched at Gibraltar, but were kept on board; arrived at Malta on the 18th and at

Alexandria on the 21st.

Of Malta he writes:

> Arrived at 3 a.m., was sleeping on deck and woke up surprised at seeing a sandy beach and many patrolling torpedo boats. Went into splendid harbour with white forts and houses built down to the sea edge. Soon many natives came about the ship and began diving for coins. Went on shore and drove about; all most attractive, especially the variety and beauty of the flowers"

On reaching Alexandria he found that no one either expected the transport nor knew what to do with the troops on board of her; so, he assumed the responsibility of moving his own twenty-five men to the Mustapha Barracks, and went himself to the Savoy Palace Hotel. Then follow days of confusion and "nothing but bad management. Are cabled to come to Gallipoli and then to stay where we are."

His state of mind is shown in the following letters:

> Alexandria, July 1st, 1915.
> Still in Alexandria and don't see much prospect of leaving. If only I could get hold of someone to get me out of this to the front, I would give a lot. Don't think our O.C. wants to leave for Gallipoli and has been telling us that he has sent cables there, but today it was found out that none had gone. We men, however, sent one this morning and I have written a letter myself to Commander Colmore (his chief). There seems little object in coming all this way to fight and then stop in Alexandria all summer. The armoured cars are a failure so far as Gallipoli is concerned, and have been shipped back as there are no roads for them there; their guns and crews, though, have been sent to the trenches and have done well at the front.

> On Transport, July 16th, 1915.
> I left Alexandria on Sunday night, July 14th, thank the Lord, and am now on my way to do something, I hope. We have had a splendid trip through beautiful islands and all has gone well. We expect to be at Lemnos today at 12 o'clock. The twenty-five men are with me. Commander Colmore arrived at Alexandria on the 13th and said that we were needed badly at Gallipoli. Those who have been there seem to think that it will take a long time to get through, and that it is the same as in France, but no one knows what is going on. I have written you a lot

of letters, but have received none from you so far. I got your cable and was glad to hear. It's cooler here now that we have left Egypt and I feel much better. There are fifteen hundred troops on this boat, comprising mostly very young fellows, so you can see Germany is not alone in taking out the young ones.

The transport reached Mudros on the island of Lemnos on July 16th. Here war-vessels and lighters crowded the harbour, all was confusion again, and after starting with the expectation of going to Tenedos they were landed in the evening at Cape Helles. He and his men spent the night on the wharf and were disturbed in their sleep by the Turkish guns shelling the beach close by and destroying some ammunition, some of the shells going directly over them. In the morning he moved his squad to headquarters.

A letter written about this time gives a graphic description of his first experiences:

Gallipoli: July 21st, 1915.
I arrived at the Peninsula on Sunday and came from Mudros on a torpedo boat, which was very *swell* indeed. This is the most wonderful looking place I ever saw, the whole ground is covered with dug-outs, and even the mules have their little shelters. The hill, Achi Baba, is only about three miles away, so you can imagine how far we have advanced. On the first day of the landing, we were further advanced than we are now; the troops, you see, had no food, water, etc., so they had to fall back after the first rush. The Turks shell the Peninsula very often, but don't do an awful lot of damage. The shells are not so large as those in France, though there are some that come across from Asia that are bigger. They are called 'Creeping Carolines,' and there is one gun called 'Asiatic Susie.' Nearly every day a certain number of casualties are recorded, but surprisingly few if you consider that they can shell the whole place.
On Monday I went to the trenches and saw our guns and the men. That is the part of this business that is bad. It is frightfully hot and the smell from the unburied bodies of British and Turks is dreadful. Added to all this there are millions of flies, and I saw men sleeping with the flies literally crawling in their mouths.
I go to the trenches tomorrow for three days and expect everything will be O.K. My fellow officers here are very nice.

RNAS ARMOURED CARS, CAPE HELLES, 1915

I hope we take the blooming hill before long, but personally think it will be some time. There are no warships about owing to submarines.

On July 22nd he went with his men to the trenches and joined No. 10 Armoured Car Squadron, on Maxim duty. His time was fully occupied now. By day there were gun positions to be shifted, perpetual sniping to be avoided, and the Turkish artillery to be watched as they sent over shells from time to time, some exploding close to the parapets. By night he was unable to take advantage of his good dugout for sleep, as matters became more active, the Turks' rapid firing began, and he had to be constantly on the alert in case of an attack. In the early morning, especially, with the change of night to day guard, shrapnel fire was particularly trying, and his men required careful attention to prevent careless exposure and casualties. He writes:

No. 1 gun position is near the sea, and at a free moment I started to the beach for a swim, but sniper's bullets stopped me.

Relief came every third day, with return to camp at headquarters. Then he swam often in the sea, visited the French camp, where he had already made several friends among the officers, and amused himself "fishing with dynamite," on one occasion very nearly falling a victim to a shark. Even at headquarters there was little rest, "once a big bomb burst in the middle of our camp."

On August 1st he writes by postcard:

Well, I am in fine health still. Have been in the trenches now six days all told. It has been very quiet (!) and we don't expect anything much for the present. I have four guns to take care of up there, with twenty-five men, and it takes all my time to look after them and I get very little sleep. It is very hot, but the swimming is fine when we get a chance to go in.

His next letter shows that he was made uncomfortable by ill-natured disagreements between his superior officers, a condition very distasteful to his nature, always averse to bickering, but he does not make much of this, suggesting more than anything else his wish for an American friend.

August 3rd, 1915.

Well, I am a bit discouraged with the organisation of my part of the R.N.A.S. One of the first things I found out when I arrived

36

was that the commander of the squadron I am in, No. 10, was having an awful row with the higher command of the corps, and when I got back to camp from the trenches on my first relief, I found that most of the Armoured Car force had gone, leaving only my squadron commander, three sub-lieutenants, myself, and forty men. We are to wait on the Peninsula for the next attack, which will be a big one, and then No. 10 squad., which has been reduced from a hundred to forty men, is going back to Alexandria for a rest. The men themselves are fine and some of the young officers are nice, but I wish I could get with real men like some of the army officers I have met in the trenches. There is too much quarrelling among my superiors and too little real punch.

Now I will tell you, my experiences. The first three days I was up at the front I had one gun position about five yards in front of our first line of trenches, and it was very exciting. We could only put the gun up at night, and as we were expecting a Turkish attack we were kept on the jump. Nothing unusual happened, however, except a shell which struck about five feet from us and knocked the parapet in. No one was hurt. There are a lot of dead Turks and Tommies, still unburied, some only a few feet beyond the parapet. They are all left where they fall in an attack, it being impossible to bring them in on account of snipers. The Turks bury their dead in their own trenches, but only about a foot deep, and sometimes a hand or some part of the body can be seen sticking out.

By the time you get this letter the attack all are talking about will be over, and I hope a success. Up to now we have not advanced any further than the first day the troops landed. If there was any real head with our show, I should be enjoying myself. My commander, when a shell came over, the other day, grabbed my arm just like a woman would. I don't mind it much, but it is a bit discouraging.

Will you send me out some food by parcel post? Canned peas, Chow-Chow, chocolate, anything; the stuff here is awful.

In another letter to his cousin, he writes:

August 5th, 1915.
Well, I have been on the Peninsula for about three weeks and am still whole and hearty and very strong.

I have been up in the trenches nine days altogether and the first three were very exciting, because the Turks were supposed to be going to attack. They had gotten 100,000 men together, with 60,000 reserves, and I have just found out that the *pasha* called the attack off. It was coming on the 23rd last. I had a great position in a tunnelled place about ten yards in front of our first line of trenches, and had they come we would have slaughtered them. I had three men with me in this place, and also three other guns I was supposed to look after. But as a matter of fact, the men know more about it than I do.

Every day we get shells down on us, as there is no place that is not under fire. But they do surprisingly little harm. Two of my pals, that I made on the trip out, have gone under, but none of my men, and but three wounded of the R.N.A.S. since I have been here. A man went mad on the beach today, and began shooting about, and they had to kill him. It's a cheerful life, isn't it? But you really take all as a matter of course, and I am quite happy, but would like some American friends here. The flies in this place are fierce. The evenings and early mornings are wonderful. I sleep out under a tree every night, while the rest are in stuffy dug-outs. Go up tomorrow for the big attack that is supposed to knock the Turks sideways. They say here that it will all be over in three weeks after this. The bombardment is to last three days.

The attack referred to was planned partly to engage the enemy's line and if possible, push through, but its main object was to concentrate the Turks about Achi Baba and divert their attention from a new landing in force which was to be made simultaneously higher up on the west coast of the Peninsula, at Suvla Bay. Accordingly on August 5th, Dillwyn was ordered to move his guns to higher ground in a more advanced position, and on the following day the battle began.

His diary tells of the battle as he saw it:

*August 6th.* "About 2 o'clock in the afternoon our ships and monitors began to shell the enemy on the heights. Most wonderful sight. At 3.15 my guns opened and fired seven hundred rounds each before the infantry left their trenches at 3.40. They advanced through an embrasure, the whole line of bayonets gleaming in the sun. Some fell as they stepped out, many as they got near objective, Turkish shrapnel being well directed; the few remaining fell back."

*August 7th.* "After quiet night, start bombarding at 8.10 a.m. and continue until 10.40. I fire No. 4 gun. In face of heavy fire our men go out in single file this time. Many fell at one spot near our parapet; some reached the Turkish trench and bending over seemed to go in head first; a few took cover behind trees. Saw one of them leave shelter, and help a wounded pal in. Could plainly see Turks—big strong looking men—working and walking in their reserve trenches, and trained my guns on them at thousand yards range. Soon they advanced in mass formation to counter-attack and I put two guns on them and fired a thousand rounds into their ranks. Still, they came on and drove our too few men out of the trench they had taken. Then their advance stopped. In afternoon I sniped them as they repaired the parapet of their recaptured trench. All day could hear sound of guns from Suvla."

The after impressions of the battle are given in a later letter:

August 18th, 1915.
Well, the attack has been made and was a complete failure here. Almost four thousand men went out and very few came back. Some monitors and ships bombarded Achi Baba for two hours. The Turks during this moved down into a gully and came back after it to their second line and massed four deep to meet our men. I was on higher ground with four guns and could clearly see our charges of the afternoon of the 6th and the morning of the 7th. The men went out in a hail of bullets and it was a wonderful sight to see them. Many of them fell close to our parapets, though a good number reached the Turkish trenches, there to be killed.

On the morning of the 7th the Turks made a counter-attack and drove our men out of the lightly held trenches they had taken. Our guns, fortunately, took a lot of them, my two guns fired a thousand rounds into their closely formed mass. Three hundred of our men were lost in a trench that they had advanced into, and I saw three wounded men behind a tree in front of the enemy's line who could not be brought in, and many dead lying on the ground between the lines.

Matters went as badly as possible at the new landing at Suvla. Losses at the landing itself were almost nothing. The troops easily could have gone directly across the Peninsula and cut off Achi Baba. But after going in five miles without opposition they got thirsty and couldn't get water, so retired. They hold a strip of the coast about a mile deep. Lost thousands of men in securing it, and now the Turks are busy digging themselves in, and again it will be trench warfare. This means that all is up. Two generals have been sent back to England on account of the fiasco.

From this description you can gather what I think of this campaign. There are a great many more Turks here than the English think. I think that probably our forces will have to spend the winter here unless everything changes suddenly. Even if we do, we won't get through to Constantinople unless very many more and good troops are sent out. The ground is full of gullies, and, by nature, so advantageous to defence that a few of the enemy can hold it against hundreds.

I am constantly in hot-water about home, as all here know I am an American, and the notes after the *Lusitania* aren't making us any too popular. Although my commander is friendly, I sometimes get furious. Fortunately, I am about to be transferred to Suvla. Squad No. 12 is coming and No. 10 is going to Alexandria for rest.

Please don't forget to send me some food; books would be nice too.

From August 8th to September 7th, he and his squadron were on fatigue duty at Cape Helles. He swam every day—often several times; explored the country toward the firing line either on foot or on horseback, and from the front trenches, frequently exposed to the intermittent Turkish artillery fire, saw still more unburied dead bodies which filled the air with a horrible stench. The food was scanty and bad, and this, with the heat, brought on an illness which lasted a few days only and was not severe enough to lay him up.

The letters following deal with this period:

September 6th, 1915.

Well. No. 12 squad has come out here to relieve No. 10 and I am going to the new landing where there is more to do. Lister (son of Lord Ribblesdale, since killed), the commander of all the Armoured Car force in Gallipoli, came with the squad. I had a talk with him, and he tells me that the arrangements about our corps are 'up in the air.' He thinks that it may be broken up, the officers and men recalled to England and given the choice of going into the Naval Air Service or into the Army.

40

He wanted me to stay at Cape Helles, but I protested and am going to Suvla. You can't imagine in what a mix-up the whole affair is. We have done nothing for a month. In fact, the whole front has been quiet and even at General Headquarters they are uncertain what to do. If they don't wake up soon, they will be the laughing-stock of the world. I wish I could write you something cheerful, but the truth is best.

September 9th, 1915.

I arrived at Suvla Bay, the new landing, on a trawler yesterday after stopping at Gaba Tepe and seeing the Australians, who are a splendid lot of fighting-men. We landed at 6 p.m. and went into camp a short distance up from the beach. All is a hopeless muddle here and things have been wretchedly managed. Our troops, as I told you before, are now farther back than they were the first day of the landing owing to their not having artillery support, ammunition, reserves, or even proper maps of the ground they were expected to occupy, to say nothing of food and drinking water. Some very stupid things were done, such as moving troops in marching formation for two miles over open ground in the daytime. Of course, they were cut to pieces, the casualties amounting to two-thirds of their number.

Three of my pals at Hythe were in the trenches on the ridge facing the Turks—Jefferson's Post—but, several days ago, two of them were wounded and the third killed, all in their dug-outs. The men I find capable and very satisfactory.

We hear again that the Armoured Cars are going to be disbanded. Word has come that there are no more reserves for us and that when our numbers are exhausted by sickness and wounds, we are to turn our guns over to the army. You can see how discouraging it is, and I really don't think it worth our while sitting here all winter doing nothing. The army doesn't recognise us, because we belong to the R.N.A.S., neither does the navy, because we are acting on land.

The nature of the country here is like that before Achi Baba, there being a big range of hills occupied by the enemy and many gullies. The Turks let us land and advance to the foot of the hills, but not a step further. They have been shelling the neighbourhood lately, and killed some men in the camp next to us; none of our men have been hurt since I have been here.

41

We have very little drinking-water here and no bread to speak of. Just Bully Beef and bacon.

September 21st, 1915.

I have had an attack of jaundice but don't feel badly at all now. The doctor won't let me go into the trenches at Jefferson's Post though I am sure I am well enough. There has been no move here for a long time, and both sides are just sitting opposite each other sending over shells once in a while.

I get no parcels and no post, though I am very anxious to hear what is happening in our world and what all my friends are doing.

The nights are growing cold but the days are warm and fine. The sea and hills are beautiful, and there are vast flocks of gulls flying about. I get, by the way, many good swims—water cool and bracing.

On September 24th his diary notes:

See doctor and get permission to go to Jefferson's Post and walk up to the trenches there. Beautiful day and sea as blue as can be. Look over gun positions and take some shots with a rifle at Turks. Have a dug-out to myself.

He writes:

September 25th 1915.

I have at last received some letters, dated 28th August and 5th September; no parcels. The one from Mrs. Morgan, enclosed, was nice to get. It had so much home news. I always like to hear what Bobby and Charles and the rest are doing.

I am now with Squad No. 11 at Jefferson's Post up in the first line trenches on the extreme left, and overlooking our whole front as well as the Turks. The Bay of Xeros is on our left and the view is very fine.

We have had a little excitement. Two of our men that I came out with have just been wounded, though not badly, and near us a trench-mortar bomb killed one man and wounded four others this morning. I have done some sniping, but don't think that I have hit any Turks, as the range is six hundred yards, and we only see their heads. The weather is still good and I feel better than when I last wrote. I was told that if I was not well enough to go to the trenches in two days I should be sent to a hospital ship, so I persuaded the doctor to let me go and I am better already. There is no progress here, and the Turks are digging themselves in deeper every day.

On the 26th he was:

Officer of the watch and occupied a dug-out near No. 5 and No. 6 guns. Inspected at 2 a.m. and found one man sleeping. At dawn, the enemy began shell fire, wounding one of our men, and killing one and wounding three of the Yorks to our right. A sergeant of the latter shot in the stomach by sniper. Hear that we are going to attack, will get it hot if we do.

Next day:

Spent the morning watching shell fire from the Anzacs. In the evening sniped at Turks. At 9 p.m. got an awful shock when the whole of our first line came into action. Took my men to front and with rifle and bayonet waited for the enemy. False alarm.

*September 28th.* "Barbed wire is being put up in front of us. Some think that the Turks are going to attack; I don't. We are very inadequately fortified if they do, no support trenches, and we will be driven into the sea if they take Jefferson's Post."

*September 29th.* "Nothing doing. No water to wash in, or for shaving. Take a walk in the afternoon down to the beach and have a swim, it was magnificent and the air and sea like home."

Of the alarm of the 27th he writes in a letter:

October 1st, 1915.

We have just had some changes. The other night things got in a bit of a panic, as word was passed that the Turks were about to attack, and if they had they would have had an easy job of it in our part of the line. There was no foundation for the alarm, and in consequence the best officers and men of both No. 9 and No. 10 squads have been sent up here while others with the O.C. of No. 11 squad have gone down to the base camp. One other and myself are the only officers of those here on the night of the false alarm, who are selected to remain. I don't think that the Turks will attack at this place now. We have barbed wire all along the front of Jefferson's Post. I believe that we shall just hold on and won't attack either. I don't hear any more of our

43

leaving. If I get a chance, I shall go to France again and, if I change, I shall pick out a really good regiment. Since writing this my C.O. has told me that they have no good officers and that I am wanted at Hill No. 10, and has ordered me to go to the base camp and report.

October 14th, 1915.

Since I wrote last, I have been at the base camp, but am now up in the trenches at Hill No. 10. We, and in fact, the whole front, are very quiet, though we are always subject to more or less gun fire. For instance, when I was walking from camp to the beach for a swim, shrapnel went over my head. A lt. colonel who was near ducked under a rock, but there was no cover for me, and three shots came pretty near, one cutting a soldier's head off and wounding three others. Early in the morning of the 6th, soon after I got to Hill No. 10, our battleships started to bombard the heights opposite Jefferson's Post and plastered the Turkish trenches with shells, doing very good shooting.

At the same time, a battery posted behind us opened upon the same target and threw shrapnel over our heads, some bursting short and very close to us. On the 11th our camp was shelled—five shots in all—killing one of our officers, and, on the next day, high explosives came over from the Turks and, later, as I was walking up to Jefferson's Post I was sniped at and forced to return. Saturday, I saw an aeroplane descend on Salt Lake—dry now—and soon the Turks began to fire at it and hit it after ten minutes' trial, knocking off the right wing. So, it goes every day. There is a rumour that the Admiralty has recalled us, but the army won't let us go as they need our guns and men.

I have received nine boxes of food all at once, and appreciate them a lot. I only wish they had come some weeks ago when I needed them more. The weather is beautiful.

October 26th, 1915.

We are told now that we are to be disbanded in two weeks. The men to be sent to Embros and the officers to have their choice of staying here with the army or going back to England. In the meantime, we are consolidated into one squadron of ninety-three men and eight officers. It is realised that we cannot be reinforced from the army and we have no reserves to draw on. Most of our men are ill and all are discouraged by the vacillating policy regarding us. Especially with the statement that has come to us that we 'are gradually to die a natural death!' I think I'll choose France.

On the 21st, after inspecting trenches, received orders to go to Jefferson's Post and walked first to the base to buy a mackintosh and then to the ridge. General Dallas of the 11th Corps, the commander of this section, has been here and ordered us to fire machine-guns on enemy during the night. Am duty officer and have a good dug-out to myself with a canvas bed and, best of all, am having a more interesting time than before. We are on the top of a peak overlooking a valley and opposite the Turks about four hundred yards away.

I take charge of six guns, as the other officers are teaching gunnery, and am responsible for a part of the line. I go out in front of the trenches at night with a patrol, to a listening post a hundred yards in front of our position; snipe the Turks and am sniped at, a lot, by them, and altogether it is very exciting. Our infantry are sent out at night to put up wire and always 'get it in the neck.' The Turks are clever and clean fighters. Two of my officer friends were hit yesterday and six more today.

Something pathetic happened last night. An awfully nice artillery officer about eighteen years old told me at mess that he was going out in the night in command of a winner party and said he didn't expect to come back. Sure enough, he was shot in the back and killed. I wonder if he knew!

To make matters more interesting our ships bombard from the harbour and from the Gulf of Xeros directly under us. We see the shells plunging into the trenches and bursting in the air over them, and at night it is a great sight. Yesterday we bombarded the Turks with field guns and Maxims, firing five hundred rounds. Artillery is being moved up to our front and I expect that we will make an attack here soon to take the ridges opposite us. This I know from experience will be a harder task than is generally thought.

November 1st, 1915.

Am duty officer up here for all the naval guns and am kept busy day and night. Have to be ready for any attack, and am enjoying myself. Things are beginning to move a bit since some new generals have come out. We bombard the Turks every day and they reply. Was hit in the shoulder by a pretty big bit of flying rock but not hurt. Am directly up in front and on top of the ridge. Have seen a number of the enemy, but, as a rule, they keep well hidden and can only be seen singly.

We are still troubled by uncertain plans as to our future. Nearly all want to be disbanded and the men are well fed up. I suppose if they want me, I shall stick it out. One of our officers—the best we have—is going to transfer to the 33rd Brigade under General Dallas.

*Later.* Was walking about looking over the trenches this afternoon, and ran into General Dallas, and he asked me to join him too, and said that he had put in a request for me. It was a compliment, but I don't think I shall, even if the Admiralty allow it, as I want to go to France again. I thanked him and told him this; but he answered that he needed and wanted me and I should soon be a captain. However, nothing can be done about it until further developments.

The weather is fine and I feel very fit. All is quiet now except for bombardments which don't amount to much. It looks as if we were about to make a push.

A few days after writing this letter, November 4th, he was attacked by dysentery, and after trying to keep going for three days was sent down to the base hospital. Before leaving he took Kodak pictures of some of those in the trench. An officer named Kirkwood jocularly told him if anything happened to send his picture back to his wife. He had only been married two weeks before he left home.

After two days in hospital Dillwyn returned to Jefferson's Post, and writes:

Arrived back at 12.30. Saw three men on stretchers, bleeding, and almost gone. One was Kirkwood. Two big shells went into the trench two hours before.

★★★★★★★★★

Kirkwood's brother-in-law, to whom the photograph was sent when Dillwyn returned to London, gave an interesting account of a Scottish tradition. On hearing of Kirkwood's death from the War Office he telegraphed the clergyman of the family parish in Scotland, and asked him to break the news to Kirkwood's father. In delivering the message the clergyman did not ring but knocked on the door. "Rapping on the door" means bad tidings in Scotland. The father, mother and wife were seated in the library, and the former went out to answer the summons. When the young wife finally heard the news, she fainted and was given brandy to revive her. Whereupon the *dominie* declared "This is no place for me," and abruptly left the house.

★★★★★★★★★★

*November 12th.* "Turks began fire at 10 o'clock; kept it up for an hour, throwing over sixty shells. A part of the first parapet was knocked in, one man was blown to pieces and three others wounded, and I helped with them. Later in day word came that I had been ordered by the Admiralty to return to London and report. Left Jefferson's Post at 2 p.m."

On November 13th, at 7.30 am, he left the Peninsula on a trawler for Mudros. Here there was some delay about transportation, but by the 16th he had secured his permits, made arrangements, and was on the *Northland* on his way to England. The voyage was uneventful. He enjoyed the sea, and the quiet and comfort of the ship, and speaks in his diary of Gibraltar and of the beauty of the peaceful Spanish coast with its little villages with white houses on the hills, and of its more distant mountains. "A place to visit again."

The coast of Wales was sighted on the 26th at 11 o'clock in the morning on a cold, brilliant sunshiny day. The latter unique in his experience, as he always had approached England in heavy rain.

4

We met him at Paddington Station, having been notified by wire of his coming, and were on the platform near his carriage when the train stopped. He jumped out, sunburned and looking very much a soldier, but after the first greeting we felt that he had changed, and this feeling was confirmed later. He seemed to have dropped much of his youthfulness, and to have become more serious and possessed by a more purposeful energy. These changes showed in his manner and in the expression of his face, while his steadfast eyes looked as if they had seen many grave sights, and, as has been said of a recent picture of him, as if one could read in them the whole history of the war.

He seemed not to care to talk much of Gallipoli, and in what he said there was little reference to the dangers he had passed through or to hardships endured. His conversation dealt mainly with the conduct of the campaign of which his opinion was far from favourable; the discouraging lack of efficiency and fixed purpose in the management of the Armoured Car Division; the good qualities of his own men; the

47

cleverness and clean fighting of the Turks, which, he thought, now that they were warned and prepared, made their defeat and the taking of Constantinople highly improbable. He spoke, also, many times of the strange beauty of the Peninsula and its surrounding sea.

Since the abandonment of the Gallipoli expedition, however, we in England have had harrowing reports of what the troops suffered. The men brought back tales of the trying tropical climate; hunger and thirst; the prevalence of disease, especially dysentery, enteric, and jaundice, and the hard life in trench and dug-out often in proximity to unburied and decomposing bodies and plagued by myriads of flies. They told, too, of the teasing Turkish gun-fire, which was able to search every trench and camp, and the perpetual sniping, both taxing their vigilance night and day; of the slaughter attendant upon attempts to advance, and the discouragement incident to the failure of attacks upon naturally strong positions made practically impregnable by the devilish ingenuity of the Turks' German masters.

Such continual looking into the face of death, under very adverse conditions, could not result otherwise than in some way markedly influencing the survivors. Of many it made nervous wrecks; of others, magnificent fighting men, as, for example, in the case of the Anzacs. Upon Dillwyn the ordeal was purely developmental in its effect. He came through it with unbroken nerve, a more thoughtful, serious man, and mentally and physically a better soldier.

When he reported at the Admiralty, he was told that he had been recalled because the Armoured Car Division was being disbanded. He was given a choice of several alternatives. Either to go into the Navy Flying Corps, to transfer to the Army and become either a pilot in the Royal Flying Corps or join any regiment. Finally, being an American, he could have left the service with an honourable discharge, but both of us quickly agreed that it would be most unfair to desert the Allies at a time when matters were going none too well for them and when they needed every man who was fit and experienced. With the two other propositions a decision was difficult.

His friend Oliver Filley of the Royal Flying Corps, who had been flying in France with distinction, and was then in London on leave, urged him to join the R.F.C. and be with him. On the other hand, Walter Oakman, who had joined the Coldstream Guards, suggested his becoming a Guardsman. It was impossible for him to make up his mind at once, so with the question undecided he and Filley availed themselves of Waldorf Astor's offer to put his shooting and gillies at their disposal, and went for a month to Scotland.

Returning to spend Christmas with us he passed a few days in investigation, and then determined to accept a commission as 2nd Lieutenant in the Coldstream Guards. This was a step down in rank, and with promotion only by seniority, but it offered a sure prospect of speedily returning to the front. The air service required more mechanical knowledge than he possessed, and an exceedingly protracted and tedious training. At the same time the unequalled status of this Regiment of the Guards met the definite resolution he had formed in Gallipoli, that if an opportunity for a change ever came, he would associate himself only with trained soldiers.

In pursuance of this plan, he went on January 5th 1916 to join the Coldstream Battalion at Victoria Barracks, Windsor, for the preliminary training imposed upon everyone entering the Regiment, no matter what his previous record. His idea was that this would be short, and he thought that with his experience in Flanders and Gallipoli he was quite prepared to go out almost immediately. But he found that what he had been taught with the Armoured Cars and later at Hythe and at the front, were mere rough outlines compared with what he was obliged to know with the Guards.

At first, he could not see why to fight well it was so necessary to be careful as to carriage, dress, and attitude to those over and under him, and to observe such watchful care of his men. Or why the knowledge of drill and other technical matters had to be so perfect. But Coldstream tradition and spirit soon appealed to him, and he began to see that the very things which, at first, seemed trifling and were irksome, were an essential part of the perfect discipline that had made his Regiment second to none, and he became proud to be one of them.

It is beside the purpose here to go into the details of the months he spent at Windsor. It suffices to say that he was well occupied with training, barrack work and guard duty at the castle, where his name, according to custom, is inscribed on the wall of the Guard-room. However, we saw him frequently in London and at Sunningdale, where we had taken a house to be near him, and where he often came for the night and for the weekend; and later, at Windsor itself, where we spent several weeks before he went out in order to see as much of him as possible and make some home atmosphere for him.

At last, he seemed to have come to his own, for his fellow officers were chiefly college men and of the same class in life. They knew that he was an American and honoured him the more for voluntarily help-

THREE COLDSTREAM GUARDS ON THE WESTERN FRONT

ing in a cause he thought right, and held him blameless for the weak policy of a government he could not control. Finding, too, that he had many similar tastes, they quickly fraternised, in golfing and rowing in relaxation hours and in the regimental football team with which he played against other regiments and Eton. For his men he always had an admiration and deep liking, and his ambition came to be, as he told a friend, to lead them in a charge.

So, the time passed until the day came for him to go to France, on Tuesday the 11th of July. We and a large party of his own friends (including Richard Norton, his chief in his ambulance days) saw him off and said goodbye at Waterloo Station, and he left us with quiet cheerfulness and high expectations. Besides himself there were four other Coldstream officers in the draft. A compartment had been reserved for them, with a lunch table daintily set, and one could not help contrasting this departure with the one of little more than a year before with the Armoured Cars from Dover.

5

The story must be continued through some of his many regular letters, for although he probably kept up daily records, no diary has been found. If it existed it was probably in his pocket at the time, he received his mortal shot.

Guards' Division,<br>Base Depot, B.E.F., France.<br>July 14th, 1916.

I arrived at Havre early on Wednesday morning and came out here to camp. We had a good trip over except for no sleep.

Yesterday I went up to the trenches and acted captain of a company. The men were, of course, strangers to me. However, I got through with it somehow. In the afternoon we were ordered to join the Intrenching Battalion near Albert, and I think it will be interesting here as we are quite well up to the front. There are Scots, Irish, and Grenadiers with us, and some of our own officers who have not gone up yet. All the men are splendid and the officers unusually nice. Saw many German prisoners—strong-looking men.

Will you tell Daniels to send me a pair of slacks (long trousers) as all the officers here wear them when they stop work. Please have them made from the same material as my new uniform. Also, will you send out my old mackintosh which will be useful. Tell Daniels to send me the bill.

Lots of love to you and the family at Amberley House.

July 17th, 1916.

I am now at a place near Bray. There are many of my old pals here. They gave me a great reception, and I am sure that I am going to enjoy myself.

There is a good deal of fighting going on, and yesterday I walked over the battlefield and into Mametz Wood. We have done awfully well to have gained so much ground as we did. There is an incessant roar of cannon and it is quite lively. The weather is rotten. Went into a *Hun* dug-out forty feet below the ground. It was all panelled up and had two stoves and glass windows in the doors. Some dead are still lying about the fields, but things have been pretty well cleared up.

Think I shall stay with this battalion for some time. I think when I go to the front, I am going with the 2nd Battalion, which I believe is the best, and the one Oak and Stewart-Richardson were in.

Address, 7th Intrenching Battalion, Guards, B.E.F.

★★★★★★★★★★

J. Stewart-Richardson, after a week's honeymoon in England, had gone back to France to obtain leave to return again to London for an operation upon an old wound received in Gallipoli. He had been in the trench less than an hour when he was killed.

★★★★★★★★★★

July 23rd, 1916.

I got your letter and also *Life*, and thanks.

I am in Fricourt, having a very interesting time as this part of the line is very active. We see the whole battle from our camp and there is a tremendous roar of guns all around us. We have very little news of our progress, but know that the Australians have done wonders; that the casualties are awfully heavy, and that matters generally are not going on as well as they might. I walked up to Contalmaison the other day and saw one of our aeroplanes brought down by the *Huns*. The Germans now that they have had three weeks to prepare have brought up men and guns and it will be hard to push through them.

Jack MacVeagh is at some place about here. My servant happened to hold his horse for him, and when he saw that he was a Coldstreamer he asked about me. He told him where I am and Jack said he would look me up. He is in the 5th D.A.C. Field Artillery.

Will you send me a small silver star for a field cap which you can get at Smith's in Ebury Street. It is like the one in my dress cap, only smaller.

I go down to Carnoy and build roads when I am on fatigue. Today I am picket officer. Lots of love.

July 29th, 1916.

I got a letter from you some days ago, also magazines and *Life* today. Have no news to tell you except that I am well and at the same place. A few of the men whom I knew at Windsor have gone up to the line. They have been here six weeks. Had I gone out with them I should have been up by now. However, I enjoy it, as I can walk all over the place.

There is still a lot doing in this sector and, as usual, the Australian troops, being colonials, have done wonders notwithstanding the fact that they have had very little discipline.

Lots of love.

August 9th, 1916.

I am now with the 2nd Battalion and have the same Platoon No. 12, that Stewart-Richardson had. We are back of the line at present, in rest. I visited some of my old acquaintances with whom I stayed in these parts before, and the old woman kissed me. I never had such a warm welcome anywhere. The French people are certainly very hospitable. It was over a year and a half ago since I saw them and they seemed awfully pleased to see me back.

This afternoon I am playing football against the Grenadier Guards. We are playing soccer and I don't know the first thing about it.

The country around here is great and I have been doing a little walking. The weather is fine and the crops which are planted in every field are a fine sight.

I can't tell you any news as the War Office has forbidden officers to write home anything even to their own families. I believe one man has been court-martialled for doing it. Not in our regiment, however.

★★★★★★★★★★

Colonel Crawford told me later that he made Dillwyn play whether he knew socker or not, and he added, enthusiastically, "He was the best football player I ever saw."

★★★★★★★★★★

August 10th, 1916.

We are moving further but don't expect to do anything for some time.

The match with the grenadiers came out a tie. I was lucky enough to make a goal for our side in the last thirty seconds. The score was three all. It was a hot day and not good for football.

It is raining now and laying the dust. I hope all goes well with you and that you are having a good time at Amberley.

August 15th, 1916.

We have moved again close to the front and have very good huts to sleep in. The weather is still fine and we have had a quiet time doing a little drilling and revolver practice. With the present strict censoring it is impossible to write you any news. I am very well.

August 17th, 1916.

Am in the trenches with No. 12 Platoon the rest of my company being in support, and there is no very great activity. I find my platoon an excellent one and every man works well. My sergeant-major, Thursfield, is a good fellow and hard worker. Can you send some cigarettes for the men? Woodbine or Gold-flake are the best. The soldiers get paid very seldom and can't buy them. I have fifty men. Don't worry about me. At least I hope you will not because I shall be all right.

August 19th, 1916.

Have just been relieved from the front line and moved to the reserve trenches and only wish that I may never get it any worse than I have this time. There was one casualty this morning when a sergeant got hit in the leg by shrapnel. It is the kind of a wound that I am looking for. The reserve trenches where I am now are pretty rotten having been blown in some time aero. This makes things interesting and if we were staying, there would be lots of work to do repairing them, but there is no time now.

We leave here tomorrow for some place behind the line and then, I believe, to another destination.

August 27th, 1916.

We are back of the line now and expect to be out for a week. I have been to an aerodrome today for instruction in signalling when attacking. I believe that we are going to have a show here soon, but am uncertain when.

Our mess is very comfortable and good, you need not send me any food.

German prisoners are coming through. They seem very young. They say we may drive them back, but that the war will end in a draw. The Germans, though, are pretty much 'up in the air' and our artillery is giving them the Devil.

September 4th, 1916.

I got your letter telling me the news and also of your visit to London. Also, packages of food, but don't know from whom.

"There is a lot doing around here now and we are under two-hour orders, that is, we may have to move at any minute. By all reports everything is going well, although the rain and mud hamper us.

I got a nice letter from Fish who tells me Park and other friends have gone down to the Mexican border.

September 9th, 1916.

We have not gone into action since I last wrote you. We have been expecting to go out at any moment, but the order was cancelled and here we are still. I suppose that we will start within the next week surely.

There is a terrific gun fire here and I don't see how the Germans stand it. They seem to be fighting hard, although we keep on gaining little by little.

Had a swim in the Somme the other day and had a long talk with a French soldier I met. He says that France will stick to the end, no matter how long. Their soldiers are strong, fine-looking men, and are doing great things. This fellow seemed to think that they have a lot of men still left in reserve. All here admire the Frenchmen, and I am glad that I have French blood in my veins.

There is not much that I am allowed to tell you. Still think that the war will go over the Winter, but a great many do not agree with me. Perhaps there will be something big coming off soon.

Owing to army regulations commanding silence, these letters, covering the two months of his final campaign, show that he was fully occupied with congenial work, satisfied with his part in a perfected organisation and happy with his companions and surroundings, but furnish very few details. These have been since partly supplied by wounded Coldstream officers and men who have come back to hospitals in England. Lieutenant Wilkinson, who will be referred to again later, furnished the following data:

> After leaving the Intrenching Battalion—a composite body engaged in field practice and made up of different units of the Guards (in this instance Scots, Irish, and Grenadiers)—Starr joined the Active Battalion at Sarton on August 4th. From this date we marched about from place to place in the Albert region. Stopping at Bertrancourt, Louvencourt, Bois de Warnimont, Beauval, Montonvillers, and Méaulte. Near Louvencourt we were in the first trenches for four days. At Méaulte we stayed from August 25th to September 10th. On the evening of the 7th September, I dined with No. 3 Company. There were six of us at table, Burn, Furgusson, Clarke, Neame, Dill, and myself. Only Neame and I are left. On the 10th we marched to Carnoy.

One of the men of Dillwyn's platoon told me:

> While in the trenches near Louvencourt, we were under a hot shell fire and we men became jumpy, but Lieutenant Starr was perfectly cool, kept a look-out for the shells, said to us that by their sound in the air we could tell something of where they would strike, and put heart into us and kept us steady. We knew then that we had a good leader.

Next come the last words! With a vein of serious purpose, they show brave hopefulness, without dread and with affectionate consideration for us.

September 12th, 1916.

Dearest Family,

We are going up in the line tomorrow or next day, so if you don't hear from me for a few days, don't worry. No news is good news, and you will find out from the War Office immediately anything happens to me, which I don't anticipate.

They hope here that we shall break through the German lines, but I have my doubts. There is a chance, however, and if we do, it will make all the difference in the world.

Your pictures are great and I am glad you sent them to me.

Am going for a ride this afternoon and a swim.

I send lots of love to you both and will write again, soon, if possible.

Lovingly,                                    Dill.

Soon after this letter was written the order came for the 2nd Battalion to go to Ginchy, from which point they, together with the other two Battalions of the regiment, were to attack and break through or drive back the Germans who were holding a strong position opposite this part of the line. As a hard battle with many casualties was expected, each company was put under three officers only (others being kept in reserve)—a captain and two lieutenants, each of the latter being in command of two platoons. For his company, No. 3, Dillwyn was selected because his O.C., Captain Burn, said of him that "his men were certain to follow him anywhere," and in drawing lots for line position he secured the choice and took for himself and his two platoons (his own No. 12 and the extra one No. 11) the advance post; support, about thirty yards behind, falling to Lieutenant Neame with the other two platoons.

This selection, by his colonel, for a command in such an important attack and the responsible position secured by the draw, pleased him greatly, and he seems to have been glad, too, that he was about to achieve his ambition to lead his men in a charge; the more as it was to be the first time in Coldstream history that the three Battalions were to "go over" together. Colonel Crawford has told me since that he was poised and undaunted and they all knew that they could trust him.

The battalion reached Ginchy rather late in the evening of the 14th in brilliant moonlight, passed through the village and went into trenches on the far side. Having posted his men, he left them to join Lieutenant Wilkinson who, being familiar with the position, had been directing the alignment of the troops, and with him and Lieutenant Fuller made a reconnaissance of the ground to be advanced over in the morning. The night was still very light and there was considerable sniping. Rifle bullets splattered about them and, sometime after midnight, Wilkinson was hit and badly wounded in the hand, rapidly becoming faint from loss of blood. Dillwyn applied a tourniquet and, having revived him from his flask, partly pushed and partly carried him, very loath to leave the front, to the dressing station well behind the line.

After returning, the rest of the night was passed in the trenches with a little sleep snatched where he stood—there was no room nor place to lie down. Neame spoke with him several times on matters of duty, but he seems to have talked more with his men to prepare them for the difficult task that they all knew was before them, and those who are left speak of his coolness and cheerfulness. Something suggested to him that there were Germans close in front, and he repeated this suspicion to his captain and twice asked to be allowed to take out a patrol to investigate and if possible, bomb them out, but was refused because such an order had to come from headquarters, and shattered telephone wires prevented communication.

To give a proper conception of the coming action it will be well to interpolate here a description of the position, as we now know it, from which the Germans were to be ejected. Directly before the trenches occupied by the 2nd Battalion of the Coldstream Guards, were some shell-shattered tree-trunks, the remains of a small orchard; three hundred yards in front of these was a short trench—where Dillwyn's instinct had placed the enemy—and three hundred yards further on, a longer trench, both parallel to the Coldstream line and hastily made by joining up shell craters, of which there were many in the artillery-ploughed fields.

Neither of these trenches were indicated on the service maps as they had not been detected by scouting aeroplanes and were probably newly created. Six hundred yards beyond them were the main German trenches, the location and strength of which were thoroughly charted and known. To the left of the Guards' position there ran a sunken road. This was bristling with machine-guns, as was found also to be the case with the two subsidiary trenches.

It was understood that at 5.40 o'clock on the morning of the 15th a squadron of "Tanks" were to advance from the rear along the sunken road and silence the machine-guns there. At 6.20 the Guards were to "go over."

True to the appointed time the "Tanks" were heard to start and, under heavy gunfire, to come on a little way. Then they stopped! Every man in the Coldstream trench realised the import of this failure. One of the non-commissioned officers spoke to Dillwyn about it and was answered "I know, but we will go on without them." From this time, piecing together the bits of the story as they have reached me, I can picture him as the fixed moment approached, full of eagerness and suppressed energy and without the slightest trace of fear, standing with one foot so placed in a niche in the trench that he could leap to the top and over at the instant time was up, and hear him say, "five minutes more, men," "one minute more, men," and "time's up."

Then, they tell me, he sprang on to the parapet, revolver in hand, and waving his stick and shouting, "Come on, 12 platoon, come on," leapt over and led on the charge. They went out into a perfect storm of shells and a hail of machine-gun bullets, a direct fire from the short trench in front of them and an enfilading fire from the uncleared road to the left. (Having depended upon the "Tanks" to take the enemy by surprise there was no protective barrage.) But they pressed on, he always well in front of his rapidly thinning platoons. They reached the short trench and here Dillwyn fell, just as he was springing upon its parapet, with his face to the enemy, shot through the heart, and killed instantly. His men, after a severe struggle, took the trench and, with the wave of support, swept by him. Less resistance was offered at the second trench, and when they reached the main trench the few who were left occupied it without any difficulty, as the Germans were on the run, and held it securely until they were relieved next day to take part in the capture of Lesboeufs.

The first report of Dillwyn's death came from wounded Coldstream officers who arrived in London on September 20th at the private hospital at 58, Grosvenor Street, where Walter Oakman was recovering from a severe wound received some months before. These officers told him of the sanguinary battle and, though not in the same company, they had the worst fears for Dillwyn. With characteristic unselfishness he, at once, got out of bed and went to see the colonel's wife to learn what she had heard. Mrs. Crawford had that morning received a letter from her husband telling her that of all the officers of his battalion who "went in" he had only brought one out unwounded. "Starr, Edmonstone and Lane killed." (Sons of Sir Archibald Edmonstone and Sir Ronald Lane.) Then he and Dr. Percival White, with much kindly sympathy, broke the news to us.

There was a slight, almost impossible hope that there might be some mistake, but the official notice reached us the next day in the following wire, which is inserted because of its considerate wording:

Deeply regret to inform you that 2nd Lt. D. P. Starr, Coldstream Guards, was killed in action September 15th. The Army Council express their sympathy.

Secretary, War Office.

Almost coincidently, accounts came through about this charge of the Guards, accomplishing its object in the face of such resistance and with the great handicap of an enfiladed flank. It roused the pride and admiration of all England. The press rang with praises of it. As one example I will quote the words of "A Correspondent" that appeared in the *Morning Post* of September 22nd.

> With the British Army,
> Sept. 19th.

When the Guards set out at dawn last Friday morning to go forward with the rest of the battle front, for the first time in the history of the regiment three battalions of the Coldstream Guards charged together—advancing, as one eye-witness describes it, 'as steadily as though they were walking down the Mall.' The line rippled over the broken ground, never halting or hesitating, while shells burst above and around them. Gaps were blown in their ranks, only to disappear as the battalions closed in again; machine-guns raked the fields over which they passed, but they could not stay the steady, onward drive of the cheering Coldstream Guards.

The Guards fought gloriously. Still the shells rained down on them as they lay in the captured trenches; still the machine-guns beat an infernal tattoo across the slope as they scrambled out to charge anew another thousand yards. Yet they swept into the second line like a whirlwind, and it was theirs! All the rest of the day they lay under a devastating fire. So, they dug into the crumbling earth and threw out their outposts, and when night fell they were still hanging on grimly, no counter-attacks could shake them loose from the ground that they had won.

As they crouched in their shallow trenches, they saw the beaten enemy falling back—saw him slinking away from the remnants of the line he had tried to hold—men, machine-guns, field guns, bomb stores, all in full retreat from the position they had tried to maintain at all cost. They had met the Guards.

While they lay under fire throughout the night some of their number brought up food and water through the German barrage. And when they were relieved at dawn they marched back as steadily as they had advanced, thinned battalions and weary, but undaunted. 'They were simply splendid; nothing could stop them,' was the tribute of one of their officers.

The details of Dillwyn's part in all this after giving his order to

"Come on" will never be fully known, though one may readily imagine his keenness in the charge and his deeds during the supreme hour—the culmination of his athletic career and war training. He was seen to "go over" and go forward in front of his men, but nothing more, by Lt. Lionel G. C. Neame, who was stricken down at the moment of ordering his supporting platoons forward.

Lt. O. W. H. Leese started abreast of him and they advanced between forty and fifty yards together, when he wheeled to the left and Dillwyn to the right, and he saw him no more. He was himself soon seriously wounded. Captain Burn, who was in the trench with him, was mortally wounded very early in the action and died in a few hours. So it is to his own men that we must trust for most of what we actually know, and although in the stress and confusion of battle even personal experiences are blurred, their letters do furnish some points, and at the same time show, how much they thought of him.

Ward D, S. G. Hospital,
Birmingham,
October 3rd, 1916.

Dear Sir,

I shall be very pleased to give you some information of your friend whom I knew so well, but I did not see him killed though we were only a few yards apart.

On the morning of the 15th I was speaking to him about the trench we had to take, in fact, it was more of a redoubt, held very strongly by the Germans, and we were the first over at 6.20. We were held up for a few minutes between our line and the Germans. He was then all right. The order then came to charge the trench, in that he got hit while leading us in the charge. I did not see him fall, but was told while in the captured trench that he had been shot through the heart. We all knew we had lost a splendid leader who saw no fear. He knew, and so did I, that we should have a terrible fight to gain the trench, but he was cool, and cheered up all his men, and I am sorry he did not live to see the spirit he had put into them in the final charge. He died a hero always in front of us.

I am very sorry, Sir, I can give you no more information of Lt. Starr. He could have felt no pain, and will be a great loss to our Company; such men so cool under a terrible barrage of fire are not so easy found. Your loss is also ours, for I knew him as a

61

gentleman and soldier on the battlefield and off.

Trusting, Sir, this information will convince you he died a hero at the head of his men, I don't think you could get better, for I was only a few yards away from him.

Yours truly,

Philip Andrews, Cpl.

1st Southern General Hospital,
Stourbridge,
Worcestershire.
October 6th, 1916.

Dear Sir,

In answer to your letter regarding the details of Lt. Starr's death. Well, I was quite close to him when he got shot. He was just off the German trench; he received a machine-gun bullet through the body, death being instantaneous. He was a fine fellow, and a braver officer never led troops in an attack. When the signal was given, he was on the parapet of our own trench with his stick in the air, you see he carried a walking stick in one hand and a revolver in the other, and it was I who passed the remark that poor Lt. Starr had got killed. He was one of the boldest and bravest men on the battlefield; any man in No. 3 Company would tell you the same.

It seems rather a coincidence, but as it happened, I think I was the last man to receive a five-*franc* note of him, as my section won it for bombing. You see he was a very good sport and often used to have bombing competitions amongst the different platoons.

Well, Lt. Starr was killed while leading the first wave of No. 3 Company attacking from Ginchy toward a village called Lesboeufs. The attack started at 6.20 a.m., and it was while the Company was fighting for the front line trench that I was wounded. I am sorry to say also that our company officer was shot in the same charge, only he lived through his, I believe— well, he was living when I came away. His name was Capt. H. C. Burn.

Well, Lt. Starr's body lies in front of Ginchy, and I suppose he will be picked up and buried somewhere near Ginchy or Guillemont. So, I think that is all I can say. Never did a man give up his life more bravely than Lt. Starr of No. 12 Platoon,

2nd Coldstream Guards; he died a great and brave death leading his men on to an objective which I am pleased to say they got, clearing the path for a further advance. Paying heavily, but never mind, we can't expect to drive them back only by losing men.

Yours very truly,

Cpl. E. C. Mitchell.

To Mrs. Starr.

East Leeds War Hospital,<br>Klllingback,<br>Leeds.

Dear Madam,

Your letter I received on Saturday. I am very sorry that I cannot tell you how Lt. Starr was killed, as I was hit before we got to the trenches. I read afterwards, while in hospital in France, that he had fallen in action. There are a few things I can tell, and that is that Lt. Starr was one of the best officers we ever had. He was a good sportsman and did his best for all the men in his platoon. He always tried to get us good billets when coming from the trenches and always had a smile for us, and I am sure any of the men would have followed him anywhere and would have done anything for him. He was only a month or so with my platoon before I came away, but in that time, he proved himself to be a good officer and a gentleman. He knew no fear. I can say both for the few that are left in my platoon and for myself that we are very sad to lose him.

Yours sincerely,

J. Bracewell.

To the Same.

20th Divisional School of Instruction,<br>B.E.F.<br>January 1st, 1917.

Dear Madam,

I did not write to you before as I expected to be home on leave and I would have written from London, my home is in Chelsea. But owing to a new class assembling we were unable to get away. I am hoping to be home at the end of this month. Yes, your son had been in the trenches before with me, but on account of the Censor I am unable to mention the name of them or the place.

I did not 'go over' with him (Sept. 15th) as I was one of the N.C.O.'s chosen by my captain to remain behind to arrange for the 25th. Your son came over to me the night of the 14th and shook hands with me and gave me cigarettes to give to his men. He said 'I will not say goodbye, Sgt. Thursfield but *au revoir*.' He was so good to us all. I am very sorry I cannot give you any information as to where his grave is, but if ever I am in the vicinity again, I will do my best to find it.

Yours very sincerely,

S. Thursfield, Sgt.

This is the sergeant mentioned by Dillwyn in his letter of August 17th, probably with the intention of giving us the name of a reliable man to whom to refer in case of any mishap.

6

We next come to a telegram from Buckingham Palace and letters from his superior and fellow officers. The telegram is, on the surface, a formula sent to the families of all fallen officers, but it carries—we may believe—both a recognition of service and much kindly sympathy from the heads of the British nation. The letters have a deep personal appreciation for him as a man, and for his voluntary efforts, though a stranger, to further their cause.

O.H.M.S. Buckingham Palace,<br>27th September, 1916.

To Louis Starr, Esq.

The king and queen deeply regret the loss you and the army have sustained by the death of your son in action. Their Majesties truly sympathize with you in your sorrow.

Keeper of the Privy Purse.

To the Same.

Headquarters, France,<br>September 23rd, 1916.

Your boy was killed on the morning of the 15th, leading his platoon in an attack against the Germans.

The battalion came under very heavy rifle and machine-gun fire and our casualties were heavy, but the men in his company tell me that he was shot through the heart while leading and cheering on his platoon.

He had not been with us very long, but his ability and keenness were undoubted and he met his end as a true Coldstreamer should.

We mourn his loss and I offer you on behalf of the battalion our sincerest sympathy in your great loss.

Yours sincerely,

Reginald Crawford, Lt. Col.
Comg. 2nd Batt. Coldstream Gds.

To the Same.

Regimental Headquarters,
Coldstream Guards,
Buckingham Gate, S.W.
October 15th, 1916.

I have been trying to find time to write to you for a considerable time, but as you will doubtless be able to understand we have been kept very busy here of late and it has been very difficult to find any time for writing the very many private letters with which I have had to deal personally, and consequently those that were not written in answer to questions have been very much delayed.

I particularly wish to convey to you and yours the very sincere sympathy which the Regiment specially feels for you in your sorrow caused by the death of your gallant son, who was fighting in our ranks not because he was in honour bound to be fighting, but because he considered it his duty to help the cause of justice and right to the best of his ability.

Previously to the war we had ties which kept the regiment in very friendly touch with the U.S.A., but now we are bound to you by a very much closer bond, your son, and others like him, who never rested till they were able to give us their active assistance in upholding the honour of the regiment in this tremendous War, and this will never be forgotten in the regiment, as long as its name endures.

To have voluntarily given his life as your son has done for the cause of right and in support of an abstract principle is quite the noblest thing a man could do. It is far higher than giving it in fighting to safeguard one's own Hearth and Home, and for the maintenance of the Empire of which one is one's self a unit. And, believe me, we greatly appreciate this spirit in which so many Americans are fighting on our side. But what appeals so greatly to us Coldstreamers is the way in which our American brother-officers have thrown themselves heart and soul into the spirit of the Regiment, and there are no British-born Coldstreamers prouder of the regiment than they or more jealous of its good name, and we old Coldstreamers are prouder of no one than of our American officers, and the debt that we owe them will never be forgotten.

The glory which the Guards Division has gained by its gallant fighting in this great battle will live in history, and I feel sure that any American family who took a share in the winning of that glory will be proud of the fact, and hand the story down to succeeding generations as an honourable fact to be remembered in the family for all time.

I feel sure your son is rejoicing, as he looks back with pride on what he has done, and that it would not be fair to him to detract from his happiness by letting him see that those he has left behind are more sorry at losing him than proud of the glorious death he has died.

In the name of the regiment I offer Mr. D. P. Starr's family our heartfelt thanks for the services he has rendered and the supreme sacrifice he has made for the Coldstream Guards, and express my hope that the link which has now been forged will never be broken.

I must ask you to accept my own personal sympathy in your bereavement and to believe me,

Very sincerely yours,

J. A. G. R. Drummond-Hay,
Colonel, Commanding Coldstream Guards.

From Rupert E. Fellowes,
Lt. Coldstream Guards.
Lady Carnarvon's Hospital for Officers,
48, Bryanston Square, W.
29th September, 1916.

I hope you will not mind my writing you a word about Dillwyn—whom I have come to know well in the last six months, both at Windsor and latterly with the 2nd Battalion.

It seems to me that the only great and sure comfort (and it is complete) for you must be the splendid, imperturbable, but

DILLWYN PARRISH STARR
COLDSTREAM GUARDS.

not blind courage with which Dillwyn faced whatever was to come. He had faced, long before the time came, the one great question, and was able to meet all the petty irritations, as well as all the dangers of a soldier's life after that, with quiet humour and trust and courage.

In such a fine and courageous passing there is no room for sadness.

Officers and men were equally fond of him, and they all felt that before he was an officer, before he was an American, before anything, he was a *man*, and a man whom they could trust.

From Harold Gude and R.V. B. Loxley, (Lieutenants, R.N.A.S.)
Late of R.N. Armoured Cars, Sqds. No. 9 and No. 11.

No. 3 Wing, R.N.A.S., France.
October 15th, 1916.

I hope you will pardon us intruding on your sorrow, but we feel that you would like every bit of news about your son you can get. Lt. Loxley and myself met Dill's friend Rumsey in the American Squadron here and we were going to write him when the sad news came of his death. I have no doubt that his brother officers and his men all loved him and appreciated his pluck, but not more so than those of the Armoured Cars did in Gallipoli.

Loxley and I were first with him at Hythe, training. We next met him at Suvla Bay when he was attached to us, and we went through that campaign together. Gallipoli was about the toughest proposition of the war, but all through, your son set an example of pluck and cheerfulness which kept everyone as happy as was possible. Both Loxley and I have been out in front of the lines with him, and we shared dug-outs and dangers together. It is pretty bad when one hears of one's own countrymen going under, but when a man like Dillwyn who volunteers from sheer love of justice, gets it, it hits us doubly hard.

We are only too glad that at least we can write and share a little in your grief, for we also lost in him a friend who was a good sport and a brave gentleman. The only consolation, if such it can be called, is that he died as he would have wished. He always said that if his turn came, he would like to be in the middle of the game where the fighting was the hottest.

Please accept our most sincere sympathy in your sad loss.

The next letter, from Richard Norton, goes still further back:

The American Volunteer Motor Ambulance Corps Inc.
(Section *Sanitaire Americaine*, No. 7)
October 2nd, 1916.

It was only a few days ago that I heard the bitter news of your son's death. It was not unexpected, for everyone who knew Dill, knew that he would always be in the forefront when honour called. That he and I once worked together will always be, so long as memory lasts, one of my most pleasant thoughts. No words of mine can numb the grief that you and his mother suffer, but I take a certain sad pleasure in expressing to you the honour in which we all hold the mother and father of such a youth and the keen realisation we have that we are the better men for having known him.

A beautiful and most Impressive Memorial Service for fallen Coldstream Guards was held in London on October 7th. The account I give of this is taken from the *Morning Post* of two days after.

A service in memory of the officers, warrant officers, non-commissioned officers, and men of the Coldstream Regiment of Foot Guards who fell during the month of September in the Battle of the Somme was held on Saturday afternoon at Holy Trinity Church, Sloane Street.

The following are the officers who gave their lives on the field. (Then follow the names of twenty-five officers, Dillwyn's amongst them.)

Admission to the church was by ticket, and the mourners and others were met at the entrance by the officers of the regiment, who directed them to seats reserved for them. The band of the regiment, stationed on a platform in the south aisle, played a selection of elegiac music during the seating. The full choral service, after the playing of Chopin's *Marche Funèbre,* commenced with the opening sentence of the Order for the Burial of the Dead, 'I am the Resurrection and the Life,' following which was sung the Psalm, 'God is our Hope and Strength.' Preceding the reading of the Lesson from 1 Corinthians xv, the hymn 'On the Resurrection Morning,' was given, and afterwards the impressive hymn 'Sleep On, Beloved, Sleep, and Take Thy Rest.' The following special prayer was then recited:

'Let us commend to the mercy of God the Officers, Warrant

Officers, Non-commissioned Officers and Men of the Coldstream Guards, who have laid down their lives for their King and Country. May they have eternal peace, and let perpetual light shine upon them.'

After other supplications and hymns, the congregation joined in the hymn 'For all the Saints who from their labours rest,' and then the following special prayer for the mourners present was given:

'O merciful God and Heavenly Father, our only help in time of need, look with pity on all those whom war makes desolate and broken-hearted. Endue them with patience and fortitude, lift up Thy countenance upon them and give them peace, through Jesus Christ our Lord.'

The Funeral March from 'Saul' and the National Anthem concluded the musical part of the service, at the end of which 'The Last Post' was sounded by the regimental buglers stationed in the western gallery.

Naturally the service was very solemn to us, but the reverence of the assembly which filled the church, one of the largest in London, was wonderful. And it seemed to me, when "The Last Post" was sounded, that all mentally visualized the twenty-five fallen officers with their men marching through wide-open gates into the Eternal City, and we felt that, in such company our own hero could not be lonely.

I cannot close this part of my record without quoting a few of the many letters received from English civilians with some of whom we had only the most casual acquaintance. For warm-hearted sympathy for us and deep appreciation of Dillwyn's willing and very brave sacrifice to help them, they are quite remarkable. They altogether disprove the usual American idea of English aloofness and reserve.

From a Friend,
September 22nd, 1916.

I must write you a line today as my heart is aching for you in your sorrow. I couldn't help remembering when I read the account of that terrible and glorious battle in this morning's paper, of Dill saying one evening at dinner, 'I want to be in a charge with the Coldstream—I dare say I shouldn't come through it alive, but I don't mind that if I've ever charged with them.' One can't help feeling that there's no way he would sooner have died than in this wonderful Charge. One can picture him leading his men and proving to them that in sport and battle their American brother is as gallant and brave as any they could wish for.

We English are so proud of what he has done and that he was ready to sacrifice himself for what he thought was right, and there are many people knowing you and him, who will say, 'America gave of her best and sacrificed her best. In the great war she was not behindhand.'

All this is poor comfort, isn't it, when what one wants is gone? But think how gloriously happy it is for him. He has fought his fight and won splendidly. It makes your fight the harder to feel he is not here, but it must make you proud to think how you helped him to win through and make the end a victory.

Dillwyn's remark, quoted in the last letter, coincides with what his friend Hamilton Hadden writes about him:

There is one comforting thought and that is that I am sure he died as he would wish to die. On the wall of the breakfast-room at the Club at Cambridge there is a picture of a Cavalry Charge with an officer, with sword upraised, leading his men on gallantly.

Dill and I would often get seats at dinner opposite this picture; would discuss the splendid sensations such a man must have under the circumstances, and we would always agree that if we might choose the kind of death we would have, we should choose such an ending.

It seems an unbelievable thought that he has been killed because he made up such a large part of the lives of his friends that life without him in it will be a changed thing for us.

From K. E. R.

Pride's Crossing,
October 4th, 1916.

There is little for me to say excepting that your great loss is a great glory too. To be an American who gives, not because it is duty, but as a free gift a precious son who is a great hero in so glorious a company must make one very proud.

As an Englishwoman I thank you and yours, and as your friend I, who am suffering many things because it is my proud duty to do so, send you a very understanding sympathy.

From Prof. F. C. de Sumichrast.

43, Eaton Rise, W.
September 25th, 1916.

Although a complete stranger to you I cannot refrain from a most inadequate expression of my profound sympathy with you in the glorious death of your son on the battlefield.

I have a personal interest in his splendid military career—none the less splendid because of his own modesty. As an Englishman I cannot say how deep is my gratitude to him and to you for his instant resolve to aid us and our Allies: as an officer—though 72 years of age— in our National Reserve I am thrilled by his record: as Professor in Harvard for twenty-five years my heart goes out to him and to you, for I loved our Harvard boys: loved them because I knew them well and, I think I may say, understood them.

Very, very dear to me are the days I spent in your land and among your people. More dear my memories of Harvard and Harvard men.

I plead this as my excuse for trespassing upon your grief, which, believe me, I share, as I share, too, the pride you must feel, in your son who saw at once that in the greatest battle for Freedom yet fought on earth, his place was on the side of Freedom. To the highest ideals of your great nation, and of our own, he has given his life, leaving us English his glad and proud debtors— his thankful, his grateful debtors.

Again, I pray you to forgive my intrusion and to believe that you have my truest sympathy and deep respect.

From Rev. Geo. F. Carr, D.D.

Amberley Vicarage, Sussex,
September 23rd, 1916.

May God comfort you and Mrs. Starr in your sore trial. It is no meaningless phrase for us to say we sympathise with you in your sorrow. For many months we have been sharers of your anxiety. It may be God's will that we also share your grief. Still, even as you mourn, you must be proud to have a son who died so nobly fighting not for his country but what must be accounted far higher, for the cause of Humanity and on the side of God. If we regard our own countrymen as heroes he is far more. America may be proud to rear such men.

The Rev. Doctor Carr also writes in the *Amberley Parish Magazine* for October:

> And we are sure everyone who knows them will unite in sympathy with Dr. and Mrs. Starr in the great bereavement they have sustained in the loss of their brave and noble son, who fell at the head of his men in the splendid charge of the Coldstream Guards.
>
> If we feel gratitude to our own countrymen, and honour them, we owe double honour to men like Lt. Starr. He, as an American citizen, could have stood out of this war. His country and people were in no danger, but he saw this country and her Allies fighting, as he believed, for the cause of right, and he was willing to give his life for high principles and lofty ideals.
>
> He served through the terrible campaign in the Dardanelles, and at the close might have retired with great honour, but the fight still went on, and he again threw himself into the fray.
>
> England must never forget such men as Dillwyn Starr, and America must be proud of sons of such heroic character.

From J. H. Seavorns, Esq.,
President of Harvard Club of London.

25 Grosvenor Road, Westminster,
Sept. 29th, 1916

At a recent meeting of the Committee of the Harvard Club of London I was requested to convey to you and Mrs. Starr their deep sympathy in the death of your gallant son in France.

Our admiration is great for all the brave men who sacrifice their lives in a noble cause. It is particularly so in the rare case of a man who makes the sacrifice with no ties of country to compel it. Those of us in the Club who are British are deeply touched and grateful that a young American should come to our aid, support our cause and give his life among our men.

For myself, may I say that having lost my only son in action in France, I can the more deeply appreciate the loss you and Mrs. Starr have suffered, but you will think with me that however much we may have craved distinction for our sons, nothing could exceed the glorious distinction they have won by their early and gallant deaths.

This English testimony may be concluded by quoting a letter from Geoffrey G. Butler, the Librarian of Cambridge University, published in the *Philadelphia Ledger* of October 26th, 1916. Doctor Butler writes of Dillwyn:

It was good of the boy to join our army, and over here, although we are a nation which does not often express its feeling, I think it was an event which was taken much to heart. Of course, it is cases like this which forge a tie between the two countries, and one which is bound to over-shadow any little temporary friction. He had a most interesting career; was in Gallipoli, in the Armoured Car Division, and then obtained a commission in the Coldstream Guards, perhaps the finest regiment in the British Army.

Throughout the whole war nothing has equalled the performance of the Guards Regiments. There is not a soldier on the British front, whatever his nationality—Englishman, Scotsman, Australian, or Canadian—who would not unhesitatingly and ungrudgingly give the palm to the Regiments of the Guards. They have, as you know, an extraordinary tradition, and draw from all that is finest in the country for their officers and men, so that not only their physique, which is very fine, but their morale is something quite out of the ordinary.

In their drill they have a precision which other regiments often lack. You can imagine it if you think of the drill at West Point on some grand occasion made a little less ceremonial and adapted for service needs. The discipline, alike for officers and men, is of an iron character, and I am told that even when they are in reserve, just behind the front, they preserve the same ceremonial in relieving the guard that one can see any day in front of Buckingham Palace.

A young friend of mine, describing a Guards regiment going into action, told me that though it was under a galling fire it was done with all the method of the parade ground, the ranks closing up automatically without orders.

It is a pleasant thought that this fine young Philadelphian was felt to have won his spurs worthily by such a regiment. I have heard that the regiment liked him, and that they recognized in him a specimen of the finest type that America produces, and felt the more warmly disposed toward his fellow-countrymen in that he quite unnecessarily chose, in this horrible show, to adopt such a course.

## 7

Nothing would have appealed more to Dillwyn than the demonstrations of affection and appreciation that have been and are being made by his hosts of friends in America. His classes at Groton and at Harvard, the members of the Porcellian Club, and very many others, joining in doing him honour. They have shown their pride in his courage, and their deep sympathy with his adopted cause, and have laid a debt of lasting gratitude upon his mother and myself.

★★★★★★★★★★

While the proof is being read a letter has arrived from Robert H. Hallowell, which says: "At the annual meeting, the Porcellian Club voted to send an ambulance to France in memory of Dillwyn. I was made treasurer of the fund, and I am sure you will be interested to know that one ambulance has been sent out, and I fully expect within a few days to have enough money to send a second. How we all loved him! There was many a moist eye when we took the vote at the meeting."

★★★★★★★★★★

Many accounts have reached us from those who were there of the beautiful Memorial Service for him in New York. This service to us was doubly significant and gratifying, in that it was solely and with no family promptings, gotten up by Dillwyn's own loyal friends, and perfected, I am led to believe, by the devoted, sympathetic leadership of Sidney Fish. Towards him and towards each one of those who participated we feel a profound sense of appreciation which must remain unmeasured by mere words.

The New York *Sun* of October 4th says of this service:

### Service for Lieutenant Starr
Held in Trinity Church, with British Consul' General present

Memorial Services were held in Trinity Church late yesterday afternoon for Lt. Dillwyn Parrish Starr, son of Dr. Louis Starr, of Philadelphia, who was killed in action in France on September 15th while serving with the Coldstream Guards. Many hundred friends and relatives of Lt. Starr attended the services. Clive Bayley, British Consul-General, with members of his office, were present.

The Rev. Joseph P. McComas, senior curate of Trinity, conducted the services. He was assisted by the Rev. Sherrard Billings, of Groton School. The chancel rail was banked with flowers, sent by his personal friends and from his School and College and Clubs, and a British Jack and two American flags were draped in their midst.

Upon the conclusion of the services the floral pieces were placed on the graves in Trinity Churchyard, especially on those of the Soldiers of the Revolution. One of the largest pieces was put on the grave of Lord Sterling, who fought with Washington. Other graves decorated were those of Capt. James Lawrence, Gen. Clarkson, Gen. de Peyster, Alexander Hamilton, and Robert Fulton.

Of this service the Rev. Sherrard Billings writes:

> My heart aches for you and Dill's Father. You knew of course the danger, but that did not make it less hard to lose him. I believe that God Himself is suffering with you in your distress. God does not want war and pain and premature death to go on in this world, and some day there will be no such thing. But so long as there is need for life to be risked in a high cause, it is gallant young men like Dill who will die. And I am sure that God approves of their motives and there will be no handicap for them in the other world just because they have missed the discipline of long life in this.
>
> The Memorial Service at Trinity in New York at which Sidney Fish asked me to officiate was thrilling, with the beautiful choir, the stirring organ recital of 'God Save the King,' the American and English flag's draped together, the wonderful flowers, and the great crowd of people Many Britishers were there, glad of a chance to pay their tribute to a gallant American who had died in their cause. It was a great privilege to officiate at that service, a privilege I shall never forget. And on Sunday in my sermon in the chapel I spoke to the boys of the Groton man who had just died. Dill will always be remembered here. It will be a satisfaction to see his name cut into the stone of the Chapel wall. I know how hard it is for you and his father. But as time goes on your beautiful memory of Dill will be an increasing comfort to you, and some day you will meet your boy again. And when you meet him, you will find him, I suspect, a leader still in some high cause. I have a feeling that Dill will thrive peculiarly in the atmosphere of the other world.

The next letters are also from Groton School. These and all that follow will be as acceptable to the British as theirs are to Dillwyn's own countrymen, since they express sympathy for the ideals of the allies—a sympathy which they are very eager for here and have been justly disappointed in not receiving officially. This withholding will always be our shame. It was so little to expect, but meant so much to those who are fighting and was all they wanted from us.

★★★★★★★★★★

When this was written I, with other Americans in England, plainly seeing the trend of events and worn out by disappointed expectations, had almost given up hoping for belligerent action on the part of our government. While the book is still in press, diplomatic relations with Germany have been broken off, and further, after more procrastination, a state of war has been declared. At last, we are gladdened by the sight of our flag exposed in honour and can once again hold up our heads with pride in our country. Not that the British have made our stay uncomfortable. They are far too generous and hospitable for that, and far too appreciative of any personal sympathy and assistance. We were humiliated because—The great principles now being advanced in justification of the United States participating in the war were as true and as existent on August 4th 1914 as they are today. And overt acts, and German brutality, falsehood and trickery came quickly and often after this date. But still we strove for peace, until our own ports were virtually blockaded and the Germans, as is their habit of giving away the belongings of others, offered some of our own States to Mexico and threatened us with war with Japan. One thanks God that at last we have "come in," but wishes our coming had been for a less selfish motive and had not been so late.

I have enough faith in my fellow countrymen to think that a Lincoln could have crystalized and led American sentiment after the outrage of Belgium, or after the barbarous sinking of the *Lusitania*. I believe, that at the beginning, *Hun* madness and piracy could have been curbed, and the war materially shortened, had a true Leader spoken in clear terms and followed words by deeds. May it not be over late to atone, by forceful action, for the shame of our delay!

★★★★★★★★★★

From Rev. Endicott Peabody, D.D.

I have thought often of you and Mrs. Starr since the sad news of Dill's death came to us.

We had prayers for you in the schoolroom in which Dill sat as a boy, on the evening that his death was reported, and the boys were touched by the thought that they were praying for the Parents of one of their own number (for we count the graduates always a part of us) who had laid down his life in a great cause. This thought—that Dill was fighting a great battle for freedom and righteousness in the world—must bring comfort to your sad hearts. By and by I trust there will come joy as well; but just now I can understand the feeling of pain being uppermost.

I remember Dill with much affection during his Groton days. He was 'all boy' then. Simple and straightforward and afraid of nothing. I fancy he kept these boyish qualities to the end. He must have been a gallant soldier and a delightful member of the regimental staff. Barclay Parsons, who dined with him on one of Dill's last nights in London, tells me that Dill had a feeling that he might fall in the campaign. But he was undismayed by that.

My heart goes out to you both in your distress, my dear friends. May God send you strength to endure, and the assurance of his love for you and for the boy.

From Wm. Amory Gardner, Esq.

Sunset Hill House, N.H.

I have just heard of Dillwyn's death and I want to write a word of sympathy. I have thought many times in the past months of your anxiety. Now I can only offer you sympathy in your sorrow. But it has been a gallant tale, and as time goes on you must let your pride in this get the upper hand of the sorrow. I am here with the Jack Chapman's. Their boy Victor you know was killed in June at Verdun. He was my godson and I have been with his parents a good deal this summer. It helps me a little to understand what all this is to you, and it is quite useless to write. But I think it helps a little to know that people care, and I did care a lot for Dill. And we are doing so little for this great cause, that it makes me proud when anyone who belongs to one in any way is saving all!

From Irving C. Gladwin, Esq.

You have no idea how much Dill has been talked about here— among boys who have never seen him. As you probably know, Mr. Billings conducted the Memorial Service in New York. He says the church was packed, many Englishmen with their families being present.

I shall never forget my first visit to Eton and the lump in my throat when I saw in the passage-ways the photographs and in-scriptions of the Eton boys who had met their death in heroic action. I hoped then to see the halls of Groton with such photographs, as an incentive among our boys to heroic endeavour. When George Borup died, I asked his father for a photograph of him to begin such a collection. He furnished us with one and we sent it to Peary, who wrote underneath a fine inscription signed with his name.

This is the first and only one we have. I hope very much that you can give us one of Dill for the second. It would be nice if we could have framed with it that splendid letter to you from his colonel, Reginald Crawford. Can you not ask him to make a copy of it for us?

I am going to write Mrs. Prince to do the same thing with regard to Norman, and hope to get Henry Farnsworth's and one of Bertie Randolph.

The letters you sent about Dill I have read to several groups of boys. When I had not time to finish, they begged to come to my room and have me read them all. Thank you so much for giving us all the opportunity of reading them. Everyone seems to have sized up Dill at once, and to have seen his sterling qualities.

I will close the Groton School letters with one more.

From F. P.

We believe—do we not—that it is 'well with the child' when we still have our precious children with us. We are content if they are well and happy. But surely that vital, vigorous Dill is stronger and gladder than he ever was. He would tell you so if he could.

I know you are a soldier's mother, which must mean that you share a soldier's heart, and I know it means that God's love and tenderness are with you. You may be sure that all of us who ever knew him in his little boyhood and young manhood feel near him and near you and his father in these sorrowful days, which still should have a strong note of victory in them for the life laid down willingly and gallantly in so great a cause.

## 8

In memory of him and in gratefulness to them, I am tempted to insert copies of every one of the hundreds of letters and cables received from Dillwyn's many friends in America. To quote only a few, as space permits, would be invidious. To discriminate would be impossible. But we shall always treasure them for the love they express for him, and they will comfort us so long as memory endures.

The next letter is typical of the spirit of them all:

From Sidney W. Fish.

63 Wall Street, New York,
September 22nd, 1916.

Your cable was telephoned me from Garrisons, and I have telephoned Morgan and Hollins and many others whom Dill would want to know first, though it was like putting knives into them to give them news like this. Dill's death is going to cause more sorrow here among all his friends, than could the death of any half-dozen other men.

I'm brokenhearted. I always thought that Dill's luck would somehow pull him through. I didn't need your cable to know that he died gallantly, as he was always living gallantly and could die no other way, but I've been so looking forward to seeing him back here, and to the things we would do together, that I feel a piece of me buried over there with him. Or will there be a funeral here? There will be so many of us who would like to feel that we had been there.

And Langdon P. Marvin, Secretary of the Harvard Club of New York, writes:

Harvard Club of New York City,
November 29th, 1916.

I am very much touched at the receipt of your letter and of the very graceful acknowledgment from Dr. Starr and yourself of the flowers sent to the Memorial Service in memory of your son by the members of the Harvard Club. We were there in large numbers, and I have never seen a more earnest, sorrowing, but proud assemblage of mourners. We are all so proud of Dill's record and of his splendid spirit. His funeral services were a fitting tribute to the memory of a brave and gallant soldier and man.

I have placed your acknowledgment on the bulletin board of the Harvard Club, where it will be read with real appreciation by the members.

You have the deepest sympathy both of the Harvard Club and of myself personally.

From Robert Grant, Junr., Esq.,

80 Lombard Street, London,
September 27th, 1916.

The news of Dill's death has made me feel so badly that I want to extend you what sympathy I can in your sad bereavement.

Dill's name has been a household word to me and my brothers ever since we were at college together. He was a great friend of my brother "Pat's." They roomed together and played in the football team together. During their college years and their summers, I got to know him well and the more I saw of him the more that attraction of his influenced me. He could not know how much pleasure he caused to everyone who knew him, but I am sure you knew it yourself, and that it will be a very happy memory for you to have always.

In college and out every one of every class loved him. I do not know anyone who was quite the same. He could not have died a finer death. This is very small consolation to his friends and to you and to his father. But I shall remember him all my life and am very proud to have had a friend like him.

A soldier's mother writes of him:

Oxford,
September 24th, 1916.

I hope you won't think it an intrusion if I send you a message of deepest sympathy, for it comes straight from my heart. Through my own son Caspar, (I met your son many times, and as you may imagine fell a captive to his charm. As an American I feel I have a right to be proud of him, for surely no man has ever offered his life more freely for a principle, and all so simply. The only time he spoke to me of what he had done, or might do, he said, 'No man with red blood having seen what this show is could help fighting for the Allies,' and with supreme lack of criticism of neutral Americans, simply added:

'They have not seen the show, and they don't know what Germans are like.'

You are indeed in the 'vale of misery,' but how proud you and his father must be that he as a man has fought for what we wish America as a nation was fighting for. Surely he must be very dear to our Blessed Lord for such a supreme sacrifice.

★★★★★★★★★★

Caspar Burton, Lieut., King's Own (Liverpool) Regt. American volunteer.

★★★★★★★★★★

From B. S.

10, Cheyne Court, Chelsea,<br>September 23rd.

I heard this morning the news of your son's death in that marvellous charge of the Guards.

Although I know you so slightly and only once met your son, I have a strong impulse to write to you my deep sympathy with you in your great sorrow, and to tell you how such a death stirs one's blood and makes one's heart beat with pride to know that our country has its heroes too. That your son died finely in a fine cause cannot really console your personal loss. All such talk seems to me worse than useless, but it must be something to know that he leaves behind him a record of such great gallantry and supreme self-sacrifice.

The next three letters are from American volunteers, the first two wounded and on leave. The third is from an Artillery Lieutenant who, though twice wounded in the arm, refused leave because he was needed at the front.

From Charles D. Morgan (R.F.A.)

81, Jermyn Street, London,<br>September 22nd, 1916.

I cannot tell you what a blow this news of Dill's death is to me, and how my heart goes out to you. I feel so much and yet I can say so little—words are sometimes quite inadequate.

From what I hear the attack of the Coldstream was magnificent. They all went over together—the three battalions—in one straight line, with their officers out in front, and didn't stop till they had reached their objective 1,000 yards away. Could anything be finer? They upheld the very best traditions of their wonderful past and Dill helped to do it. You may be sure he was in the very forefront and must have died a splendid example to his men.

From A. Grafton Chapman (R.F.A.)

Red Barracks, Weymouth,<br>Sept. 23rd.

Stuart Montgomery has just told me of Dill's glorious death. It is terribly hard I know, but it has to be sometimes, when one is fighting for the right ideas. All I can say is that I am, I hope, going out again before so very long and I assure you that when I do, Dill will be always in my thoughts and God help the *Hun* that I get my hands on. You can't imagine how we all love Dill, and I cannot tell you what his loss means to me.

From John H. MacVeagh (R.F.A.)

Somewhere in France,
October 1st.

Your letter telling me the very sad news has just arrived. I can't tell you how frightfully sorry I am for I got to regard Dill as one of my very best friends. I wish I might be with you now. The night of the big attack I had been F.O.O.; I was returning, and as the *Huns* still held out in front of the trench had to make a detour, and landed in an old *Boche* trench that had been captured by the Guards about an hour or so before. As there were two of us, we thought it only decent to take back somebody with us, for it was still too warm for any stretcher-bearers. We hunted up a stretcher and with the aid of a wandering *Boche* whom we came across got our man safely back. Oh! how I wish that our wounded Guardsman might have been Dill. As soon as I heard more, I asked permission to go and look up the Guards, but as I had been detailed to take two guns up into a forward position in the small hours of the morning, and it was already evening, my C.O. would not let me off. (MacVeagh has since received the *Croix de Guerre* for gallant reconnoitring service.) Thank you for the way you let Mother know that I had been reported wounded. I was offered a few days' leave but refused it. If you go home, I shall miss you very much for you have been more than kind to me, and should I pull through I want to pay my first visit to you. If not, may I pass out half as worthily and in just a little of the blaze of glory that he did.

In addition to these letters, I have one from Capt. Oliver Filley, R.F.C., who flew from his aerodrome in France, and with much sympathetic interest visited the battalion—or what was left of it—to question his men regarding Dillwyn. I have already quoted the details he acquired.

Under the heading "Flaming American Spirits Extinguished in the War," Eliot Norton and William P. Clyde, jr., wrote to the Philadelphia *Public Ledger* of October 28th, 1916:

Johnny Poe of Princeton was the first American football player to fall in Europe, and now Dillwyn Starr, Harvard's famous quarterback for four years, has met his death.

Strange that these two famous American football players should die, one of them holding a commission in the Black Watch, and the other in the Coldstream Guards.

The wildest guesser of their fortunes present at their birth would never have dreamed of that.

Dillwyn Parrish Starr's death will bring sorrow to his parents and regret to all who knew him. He was a singularly vivid person, intensely happy in action, taking with him wherever he went high spirits, light and motion—three lovely things. A dull grey life was not for him. When under fire for the first time he turned to his companion with an eager 'Isn't it great?'

With passion and persistence, he pursued Romance.

Then follows a summary of his war work, and:

Thus, for two glorious years he had obtained all that his romance-loving nature could demand. He experienced all the great adventures of war and finally a month ago met the greatest of them all—death in battle.

So, he lived and died in a manner fully suitable to his nature. Such a one can be truly said to be a happy man. But a bright and flaming spirit has been extinguished and to those who knew him the world has grown darker."

9

So ends this war story. The story of an American, who was true to the republican ideals of his own country, while he felt the call of his English and French ancestry, and nobly answered. A soldier, generous, and ignorant of fear. A friend, gentle, loyal, and vividly alive. A son, who was full of affectionate and protective consideration; whose whole life, from early boyhood, teemed with interest, and whose gallant passing fills us with pride.

The following lines from *Translations*, Edited by S. C, Oxford, might almost have been written of him:

Between our trenches and the enemy his body lies. We cannot rescue it, but neither can the enemy molest it. He sleeps undisturbed by the shells that hurtle over him, and well content, for he fell in the accomplishment of the task in which he excelled, and in the last of his many perilous hours it was joy he found and not fear.

# The Battle of the Somme, 1916: Third Stage

By John Buchan

The capture of Guillemont on 3rd September meant the end of the German second position on the whole front between Thiepval and Estrées. The Allies were faced with a new problem, to understand which it is necessary to consider the nature of the defences still before them and the peculiar configuration of the country.

The advance of 1st July had carried the first enemy lines on a broad front, but the failure of the attack between Gommecourt and Thiepval had made the breach eight miles less than the original plan. The advance of 14th July gave us the second line on a still narrower front—from Bazentin-le-Petit to Longueval. The danger now was that the Allied thrust, if continued, might show a rapidly-narrowing wedge which would result in the formation of a sharp and precarious salient. Accordingly, Sir Douglas Haig broadened the breach by striking out to left and right, capturing first Pozieres and the high ground at Mouquet Farm, and then—on his other flank—Guillemont and Ginchy. These successes made the gap in the second position some seven miles wide, and brought the British front in most places to the highest ground, from which direct observation was obtainable over the lower slopes and valley pockets to the east. We did not yet hold the complete crown of the ridge, though at Mouquet Farm and at High Wood we had positions which no superior height commanded.

The German third position had at the beginning of the battle been only in embryo. Before the attack of 14th July, it had been more or less completed, and by the beginning of September it had been greatly elaborated and a fourth position prepared behind it. It was based on a string of fortified villages which lie on the reverse slopes of the main ridge—Courcelette, Martinpuich, Flers, Lesboeufs, and Morval. Behind it was an intermediate line, with Le Sars, Eaucourt l'Abbaye, and Gueudecourt as strong positions in it; and further back a fourth position, which lay just west of the Bapaume-Peronne road, covering the villages of Sailly-Saillisel and Le Transloy. This was the line protecting Bapaume; the next position, at this moment only roughly sketched out, lay well to the east of that town.

Since the battle began the Germans had, up to the second week in September, brought sixty-one divisions into action in the Somme area; seven had been refitted and sent in again; on 14th September they were holding the line with fifteen divisions—which gives us fifty-three as the number which had been used up. The German losses throughout had been high. The French casualties had been singularly light—for they had fought economically under close cover of their guns, and had had, on the whole, the easier tactical problem to face. The British losses had been, beyond doubt, lower than those of the enemy, and our most conspicuous successes, such as the advance of 1st July south of Thiepval and the action of 14th July, had been achieved at a comparatively small cost. Our main casualties arose from the failure north of Thiepval on the first day, and the taking of desperately defended and almost impregnable positions like Delville Wood and Guillemont.

In the ten weeks' battle the enemy had shown many ups and downs of strength. At one moment his whole front would appear to be crumbling; at another the arrival of fresh batteries from Verdun and new troops would solidify his line. The effort had strained his capacity to its full. He had revived the old First Army—which had been in abeyance since the preceding spring—and given it to von Below north of the Somme, while the Second Army, now under von Gallwitz, held the front south of the river. He had placed the Crown Prince of Bavaria, commanding the Sixth Army, in charge of the sector comprising his own and the First and Second Armies.

He had followed the British plan of departing from the corps system and creating groups, through which a large number of divisions, drawn from many corps, were successively passed. He had used in his defence the best fighting material he possessed. During those ten weeks almost all the most famous German units had appeared on the Somme—the cream of the Bavarian troops, the Fifth Brandenburgers, and every single division of the Guard and Guard Reserve Corps.

In the early days of September there was evidence that the enemy was in no very happy condition. The loss of Ginchy and Guillemont

BRITISH "TANKS" IN ACTION

had enabled the British to come into line with the left wing of Fayolle's great advance, while the fall of certain vital positions on the Thiepval Ridge gave us observation over a great space of country and threatened Thiepval, which was the pivot of all the German defence in the northern section of the battleground. The Allied front north of the Somme had the river as a defensive flank on its right, and might presently have the Ancre to fill the same part on its left.

Hence the situation was ripe for a further thrust which, if successful, might give our advance a new orientation. If the German third line could be carried it might be possible to strike out on the flanks, repeating on a far greater scale the practice already followed. Bapaume itself was not the objective, but a thrust north-eastward across the Upper Ancre, which might get behind the great slab of unbroken enemy positions from Thiepval northwards. That would be the ultimate reward of a complete success; in the meantime, our task was to break through the enemy's third line and test his powers of resistance.

It seemed a propitious moment for a concerted blow. The situation on the whole front was good. Fayolle's left wing had won conspicuous successes and had their spirits high, while Micheler was moving his pincers towards Chaulnes and playing havoc with the main German lateral communications. Elsewhere in Europe things went well for the Allies. On 28th August Rumania had entered the war and her troops were pouring into Transylvania. As it happened, it was a premature and fruitless movement, but it compelled Germany to take instant steps to meet the menace.

There had been important changes in the German Higher Commands, and it might reasonably be assumed that von Hindenburg and von Ludendorff were not yet quite at ease in the saddle. Brussilov was still pinning down the Austro-German forces on the Russian front, and Sarrail had just begun his serious offensive in the Balkans. In the event of a real debacle in the West the enemy might be hard pressed to find the men to fill the breach. Every action, it should be remembered, is a packet of surprises. There is an immediate local objective, but on success any one of twenty consequences may follow. The wise commander cannot count on any of these consequences, but he must not neglect them in his calculations. If the gods send him good fortune, he must be ready to take it, and he naturally chooses a season when the gods seem propitious.

On Tuesday, 12th September, a comprehensive bombardment began all along the British front from Thiepval to Ginchy. The whole of

BRITISH SHELLS BURSTING ON GERMAN TRENCHES

Sir Henry Rawlinson's Fourth Army was destined for the action, as well as the right corps—the First Canadian—of the Fifth Army, while on the left of the battle to another division was allotted a preliminary attack, which was partly in the nature of a feint and partly a necessary preparatory step. The immediate objective of the different units must be clearly noted. On the left of the main front one Canadian division was directed against Courcelette. On their right a division of the New Army—that Scottish division which had won high honour at Loos—had for its task to clear the remains of the old Switch line and encircle Martinpuich, but not—on the first day at any rate—to attempt the capture of what was believed to be a most formidable stronghold.

Going south, two Territorial divisions—Northumbrian and London—had to clear High Wood. On their right the New Zealanders had Flers as their objective, while two divisions of the New Army had to make good the ground east and north of Delville Wood. Next to them the Guards and a division of the old Regulars were to move north-east from Ginchy against Lesboeufs and Morval, while on the extreme right of the British front another division of London Territorials were to carry Bouleaux Wood and form a defensive flank.

It had been agreed between Sir Douglas Haig and General Foch that Combles should not be directly attacked, but pinched by an advance on both sides of it. This advance was no easy problem, for, in Sir Douglas Haig's words:

> The line of the French advance was narrowed almost to a defile by the extensive and strongly fortified wood of St. Pierre Vaast on the one side, and on the other by the Combles valley.

The closest co-operation was necessary to enable the two Commands to solve a highly intricate tactical problem.

The British force to be used in the new advance was for the most part fresh. The Guards had not been in action since Loos the previous September, the Canadians were new to the Somme area, while it was the first experience of the New Zealanders on the Western front. Two of the divisions had been some considerable time already in the front trenches, but the others had been brought up for the purpose only a few days before. All the troops were of the best quality, and had a proud record behind them. More perhaps than any other part of the battle this was an action of the British *corps d'élite*.

In this stage, too, a new weapon was to be used. The "tanks," officially known as "Machine-gun Corps, Heavy Section," had come out from home some time before, and had been parked in secluded spots at the back of the front. The world is now familiar with descriptions and pictures of those strange machines, which, shaped like monstrous toads, crawled imperturbably over wire and parapets, butted down houses, shouldered trees aside, and humped themselves over the stoutest walls. They were an experiment which could only be proved in practice, and the design in using them at this stage was principally to find out their weak points, so as to perfect their mechanism for the future. Their main tactical purpose was to clear out redoubts and nests of machine-guns which, as we had found to our sorrow at Loos, might hang up the most resolute troops.

For this object they must precede the infantry attack, and the task of assembling them before the parapets were crossed was fraught with difficulty, for they were neither silent nor inconspicuous. The things had been kept a profound secret, and until the very eve of the advance few in the British army had even heard of them.

On 14th September, the day before our attack, some of them were seen by German aeroplanes, and the German troops were warned that the British had some strange new engine. Rumours also seem to have reached Germany five or six weeks earlier, for orders had been issued to supply the soldiers with a special kind of armour-piercing bullet. But as to the real nature of the device the Germans had no inkling.

On the night of Thursday, the 14th, the Fifth Army carried out their preliminary task. On a front of a thousand yards south-east of Thiepval a brigade of the New Army stormed the Hohenzollern trench and the strong redoubt which the Germans called the "*Wunderwerk*," taking many prisoners and themselves losing little. The fame of this enterprise has been somewhat obscured by the great advance which followed, but it was a most workmanlike and skilful performance, and it had a real effect on the subsequent battle. It deceived the enemy as to the exact terrain of the main assault, and it caused him to launch a counter-attack in an area which was part of the principal battle-ground, with the result that our left wing, after checking his attack, was able to catch him on the rebound.

The morning of Friday, 15th September, was perfect autumn weather, with a light mist filling the hollows and shrouding the slopes. At 6 a.m. the British bombardment, which had now lasted for three days, rose to the fury of hurricane fire. The enemy had a thousand guns of all calibres massed against us, and his defences consisted of a triple line of entrenchments and a series of advanced posts manned by machine-guns. Our earlier bombardment had cut his wire and destroyed many of his trenches, besides hampering greatly his bringing up of men, rations, and shells. The final twenty minutes of intense fire, slowly creeping forward with our infantry close under its shadow, pinned him to his positions and interfered with his counter-barrage. To an observer it seemed that the deafening crescendo all round the horizon was wholly British.

At twenty minutes past six our men crossed the parapets and moved forward methodically towards the enemy. The Germans, manning their trenches as our guns lengthened, saw through the thin mist inhuman shapes crawling towards them, things like gigantic slugs, spitting fire from their mottled sides. They had been warned of a new weapon, but what mortal weapon was this terror that walked by day? And ere they could collect their dazed wits the British bayonets were upon them.

On the left and centre the attack was instantly successful. The Canadians, after beating off the German counter-attack, carried Courcelette in the afternoon. In this advance French-Canadian troops played a distinguished part in winning back some miles of French soil for their ancient motherland. On their right the Scottish division, which had already been six weeks in line, performed something more than the task allotted it. The capture of Martinpuich was not part of the programme of the day's operations, but the Scots pushed east and west of the village, and at a quarter past five in the evening had the place in their hands. Farther south there was fierce fighting in the old cockpit of High Wood.

It was two months since we had first effected an entrance into its ill-omened shades, but we had been forced back, and for long had to be content with its southern corner. The strong German third line—which ran across its northern half on the very crest of the ridge—and the endless craters and machine-gun redoubts made it a desperate nut to crack. We had pushed out horns to east and west of it, but the northern stronghold in the wood itself had defied all our efforts. It was held on that day by troops of the 2nd Bavarian Corps, and the German ranks have shown no better fighting stuff. Our first attack failed, but on a second attempt the London Territorials, a little after noon, swept the place clear, though not without heavy losses.

Beyond them the New Zealand Division, with a New Army Division on its right, carried the Switch line and took Flers with little trouble. They were preceded by a tank, which waddled complacently

94

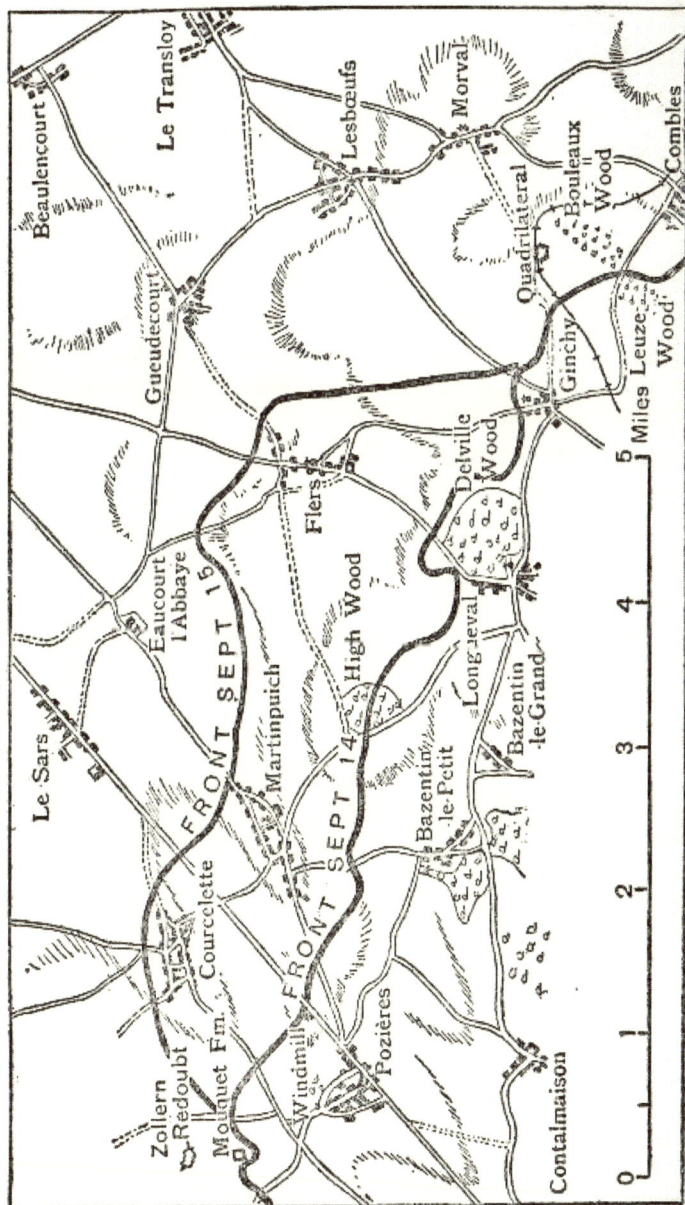

BATTLE OF THE SOMME.—THE BRITISH ATTACK ON SEPTEMBER 15.

up the main street of the village, with the enemy's bullets rattling harmlessly off its sides, followed by cheering and laughing British troops. Farther south we advanced our front for nearly a mile and a half. A light division of the New Army, debouching from Delville Wood, cleared Mystery Corner on its eastern side before the general attack began, and then with splendid *élan* pushed forward north of Ginchy in the direction of Lesboeufs.

Only on the right wing was the tale of success incomplete. Ginchy, it will be remembered, had been carried by Irish troops on 9th September, but its environs were not yet fully cleared, and the enemy held the formidable point known as the Quadrilateral. This was situated about 700 yards east of Ginchy at a bend of the Morval road, where it passed through a deep wooded ravine. One of the old Regular divisions was directed against it, with the Guards on their left and the London Territorials on their right. The business of the last-named was to carry Bouleaux Wood and form a defensive flank north of Combles, while the Guards were to advance from Ginchy on Lesboeufs.

But the strength of the Quadrilateral foiled the plan. The Londoners did indeed enter Bouleaux Wood, but the division on their left was fatally hung up in front of the Quadrilateral, and this in turn exposed the right flank of the Guards. The Guards Brigades advanced, as they have always advanced, with perfect discipline and courage. But both their flanks were enfiladed; the front of attack was too narrow; the sunken road before them was strongly held by machine-guns; they somewhat lost direction; and, in consequence, no part of our right attack gained its full objective. There, and in High Wood, we incurred most of the casualties of the day. The check was the more regrettable since complete success in this area was tactically more important than elsewhere.

But after all deductions were made the day's results were in a high degree satisfactory. We had broken in one day through three of the enemy's main defensive systems, and on a front of over six miles had advanced to an average depth of a mile. It was the most effective blow yet dealt at the enemy by British troops. It gave us not only the high ground between Thiepval and the Combles valley, but placed us well down the forward slopes. The official summary said:

> The damage to the enemy's morale, is probably of greater consequence than the seizure of dominating positions and the capture of between four and five thousand prisoners.

Three famous Bavarian divisions had been engaged and completely shattered, and the whole enemy front thrown into a state of disorder.

The tanks had, for a new experiment, done wonders. Some of them broke down on the way up, and, of the twenty-four which crossed the German lines, seven came to grief early in the day. The remaining seventeen did brilliant service, some squatting on enemy trenches and clearing them by machine-gun fire, some flattening out uncut wire, others destroying machine-gun nests and redoubts or strong points like the sugar factory at Courcelette. But their moral effect was greater than the material damage they wrought. The sight of those deliberate impersonal engines ruthlessly grinding down the most cherished defences put something like panic into troops who had always prided themselves upon the superior merit of their own fighting "machine."

Beyond doubt, too, the presence of the tanks added greatly to the zeal and confidence of our assaulting infantry. An element of sheer comedy was introduced into the grim business of war, and comedy is dear to the heart of the British soldier. The crews of the tanks—which they called His Majesty's Landships—seemed to have acquired some of the light-heartedness of the British sailor. Penned up in a narrow stuffy space, condemned to a form of motion compared with which that of the queasiest vessel was steady, and at the mercy of unknown perils, these adventurers faced their task with the zest of a boy on holiday. With infinite humour they described how the enemy had surrounded them when they were stuck, and had tried in vain to crack their shell, while they themselves sat laughing inside.

In the achievements of the day our aircraft nobly co-operated. They destroyed thirteen hostile machines and drove nine more in a broken condition to ground. They bombarded enemy headquarters and vital points on all his railway lines. They destroyed German kite balloons and so put out the eyes of the defence. They guided our artillery fire and they brought back frequent and accurate reports of every stage in the infantry advance. Moreover, they attacked both enemy artillery and infantry with their machine-gun fire from a low elevation. Such performances were a proof of that resolute and exalted spirit of the offensive which inspired all arms of the service.

In the week of the action on the whole Somme battle-ground only fourteen enemy machines managed to cross our lines, while our airplanes made between two thousand and three thousand flights far behind the German front.

In the Guards' advance, among many other gallant and distin-

97

HIGHLAND BRIGADE RELIEVED FROM DUTY AFTER THE CAPTURE OF MARTINPUICH

guished officers, there fell one whose death was, in a peculiar sense, a loss to his country and the future. Lieutenant Raymond Asquith, of the Grenadier Guards, the eldest son of the British Prime Minister, died while leading his men through the fatal enfilading fire from the corner of Ginchy village. In this war the gods took toll of every rank and class. Few generals and statesmen in the Allied nations but had to mourn intimate bereavements, and de Castelnau had given three sons for his country. But the death of Raymond Asquith had a poignancy apart from his birth and position, and it may be permitted to one of his oldest friends to pay his tribute to a heroic memory.

A scholar of the ripe Elizabethan type, a brilliant wit, an accomplished poet, a sound lawyer—these things were borne lightly, for his greatness was not in his attainments but in himself. He had always a curious aloofness towards mere worldly success. He loved the things of the mind for their own sake—good books, good talk, the company of old friends—and the rewards of common ambition seemed to him too trivial for a man's care. He was of the spending type in life, giving freely of the riches of his nature, but asking nothing in return. His carelessness of personal gain, his inability to trim or truckle, and his aloofness from the facile acquaintanceships of the modern world made him incomprehensible to many, and his high fastidiousness gave him a certain air of coldness. Most noble in presence, and with every grace of voice and manner, he moved among men like a being of another race, scornfully detached from the common struggle; and only his friends knew the warmth and loyalty of his soul.

At the outbreak of war, he joined a Territorial battalion, from which he was later transferred to the Grenadiers. More than most men he hated the loud bellicosities of politics, and he had never homage to the deities of the crowd. His critical sense made him chary of enthusiasm, and it was no sudden sentimental fervour that swept him into the army. He saw his duty, and, though it meant the shattering of every taste and interest, he did it joyfully, and did it to the full. For a little he had a post on the Staff, but applied to be sent back to his battalion, since he wished no privileges. In the Guards he was extraordinarily happy, finding the same kind of light-hearted and high-spirited companionship which had made Oxford for him a place of delectable memories.

He was an admirable battalion officer, and thought seriously of taking up the army as his profession after the war, for he had all the qualities which go to the making of a good soldier. In our long roll of honour, no nobler figure will find a place. He was a type of his coun-

MARTINPUICH MAIN STREET

try at its best—shy of rhetorical professions, austerely self-respecting, one who hid his devotion under a mask of indifference, and, when the hour came, revealed it only in deeds. Many gave their all for the cause, but few, if any, had so much to give. He loved his youth, and his youth has become eternal. Debonair and brilliant and brave, he is now part of that immortal England which knows not age or weariness or defeat.

Meanwhile the French had not been idle. On Wednesday, 13th September, two days before the British advance, Fayolle carried Courchesne east of the Bapaume-Peronne road, taking over two thousand prisoners. He was now not three miles from the vital position of Mont St. Quentin—the key of Peronne—facing it across the little valley of the Tortille. Next day the French had the farm of Le Priez, south-east of Combles, and on the afternoon of Sunday, the 17th, south of the Somme their right wing carried the remainder of Vermandovillers and Berny, and the intervening ground around Deniécourt. The following day Deniécourt, with its strongly fortified park, was captured. This gave them the whole of the Berny-Deniécourt plateau, commanding the lower plateau where stood the villages of Ablaincourt and Pressoire, and menaced Barleux—the pivot of enemy resistance south of the river.

For the next week there was a lull in the main operations while the hammer was swung back for another blow. On the 16th the 45th German Reserve Division counter-attacked the Canadians at Courcelette, and the 6th Bavarian Division, newly arrived, struck at the New Zealanders at Flers. Both failed, and south of Combles the fresh troops of the German 18th Corps succeeded no better against the French. The most vigorous counter-strokes were those which the Canadians received, and which were repeated daily for nearly a week. Meantime, on Monday, the 18th, the Quadrilateral was carried—carried by the division which had been blocked by it three days before. It was not won without a heavy fight at close quarters, for the garrison resisted stoutly, but we closed in on it from all sides, and by the evening had pushed our front five hundred yards beyond it to the hollow before Morval.

The week was dull and cloudy, and from the Monday to the Wednesday it rained without ceasing. But by the Friday it had cleared, though the mornings were now thick with autumn haze, and we were able once more to get that direct observation and aerial reconnaissance which is an indispensable preliminary to a great attack. On Sunday, the 24th, our batteries opened again, this time against the uncaptured points in the German third line like Morval and Lesboeufs, against

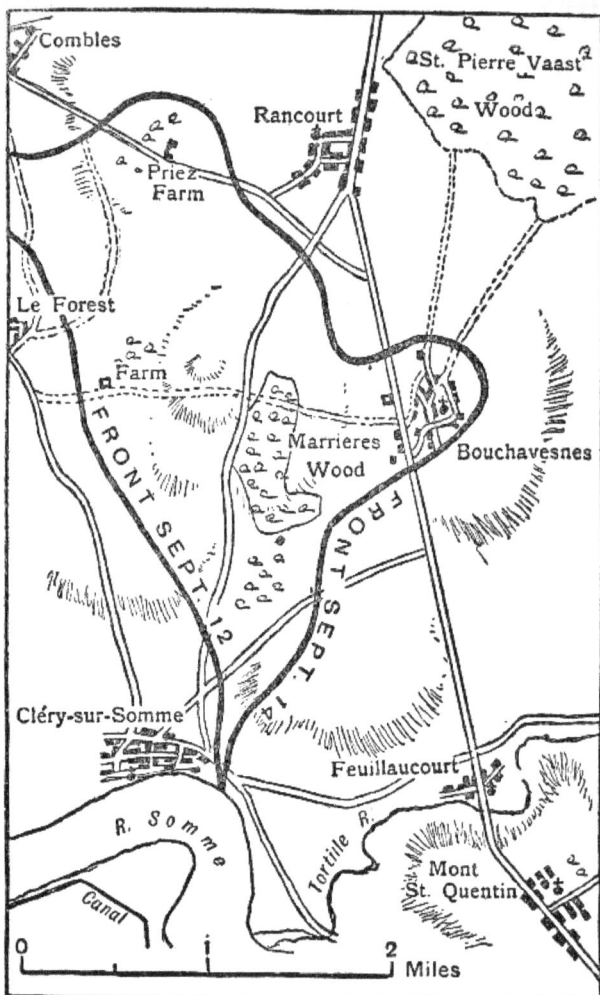

Combles

St. Pierre Vaast
Wood

Rancourt

Priez
Farm

Le Forest

Farm

Marrieres
Wood

Bouchavesnes

FRONT SEPT 12

FRONT SEPT 14

Cléry-sur-Somme

Feuillaucourt

R. Somme

Tortille R.

Canal

Mont
St. Quentin

0   1   2   Miles

BATTLE OF THE SOMME.—THE FRENCH ADVANCE OF SEPTEMBER 12-14
(CAPTURE OF BOUCHAVESNES AND LE PRIEZ FARM).

intermediate positions like Gueudecourt, and especially against Thiepval, which we now commanded from the east. On that day, too, our aircraft destroyed six enemy machines and drove three more to earth. The plan was for an attack by the Fourth Army on Monday, the 25th, with—on its left wing—small local objectives; but, on the right and centre, aiming at completing the captures which had been the ultimate objectives of the advance of the 15th. The following day the right wing of the Fifth Army would come into action, and it was hoped that from Thiepval to Combles the enemy would be driven back to his fourth line of defence and our own front pushed up well within assaulting distance.

The hour of attack on the 25th was fixed at thirty-five minutes after noon. It was bright, cloudless weather, but the heat of the sun had lost its summer strength. That day saw an advance the most perfect yet made in any stage of the battle, for in almost every part of the field we won what we sought. The extreme left of the 3rd Corps was held up north of Courcelette, but the remaining two divisions carried out the tasks assigned to them. So did the centre and left divisions of the 15th Corps, while part of the right division managed to penetrate into Gueudecourt, but was compelled to retire owing to the supporting brigade on its flank being checked by uncut wire.

The 14th Corps succeeded everywhere. The Guards, eager to avenge their sufferings of the week before, despite the heavy losses on their left, swept irresistibly upon Lesboeufs. South of them a Regular division took Morval—the village on the height north of Combles which, with its subterranean quarries and elaborate trench system, was a most formidable stronghold. The London Territorials on their right formed a defensive flank facing south from Bouleaux Wood. Combles was now fairly between the pincers. It might have fallen that day, but the French attack on Frégicourt failed, though they carried the village of Rancourt on the Bapaume-Peronne road.

By the evening of the 25th the British had stormed an enemy front of six miles between Combles and Martinpuich to a depth of more than a mile. The fall of Morval gave them the last piece of uncaptured high ground on that backbone of ridge which runs from Thiepval through High Wood and Ginchy. The next day we reaped in full the fruit of these successes. The division of the New Army which had entered Gueudecourt the day before—but had failed to maintain their ground, now captured the famous Gird trench, assisted by a tank and an aeroplane—which attacked the enemy with machine-gun fire—

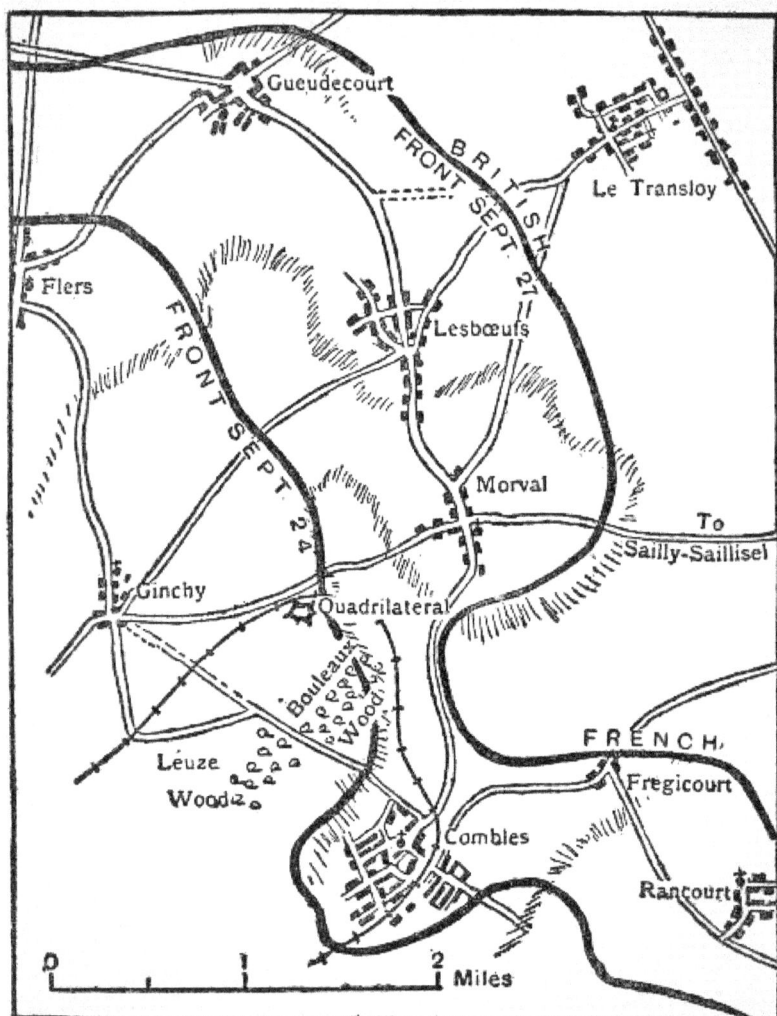

BATTLE OF THE SOMME.—THE ATTACK OF SEPTEMBER 25 AND 26 (THE GAINS ON THE RIGHT).

and by the afternoon had the village in their hands.

★★★★★★★★★★

The official dispatch thus describes this incident: "In the early morning a 'tank' started down the portion of the trench held by the enemy from the north-west, firing its machine-guns, and followed by bombers. The enemy could not escape, as we held the trench at its southern end. At the same time an aeroplane flew down the length of the trench, also firing a machine-gun at the enemy holding it. These then waved white handkerchiefs in token of surrender, and when this was reported by the aeroplane the infantry accepted, the surrender of the garrison. By 8.30 a.m. the whole trench had been cleared, great numbers of the enemy had been killed, and eight officers and 362 other ranks made prisoners. Our total casualties amounted to five."

★★★★★★★★★★

This division was one which had suffered disaster at Loos a year before on that very day, and had, since the beginning of the Somme battle, shown itself resistless in attack. It had already, played a large part in the capture of Fricourt; it had cleared Mametz Wood, and it had taken Bazentin-le-Petit Wood on 14th July. It now crowned a brilliant record by the capture of Gueudecourt and an advance to within a mile of the German fourth position. That day, too, the French took Frégicourt, and Combles fell. The enemy had evacuated it, and, though great stores of material were taken in its catacombs, the number of prisoners was small.

★★★★★★★★★

The French 1st Corps entered the line north of the Somme on 23rd August. At the end of six weeks, when they were relieved, they had taken the remainder of Maurepas, and the villages of Le Forest, Bouchavesnes, Rancourt, Frégicourt, and Combles, together with 4,000 prisoners, 23 guns, and 70 machine-guns. They believed that they had inflicted at least 40,000 casualties on the enemy. They had the satisfaction of breaking up two divisions of the Prussian Guard, and of advancing two miles on a front of six.

★★★★★★★★★★

Meantime, on the British left the success was not less conspicuous. Two divisions of the New Army, advancing at twenty-five minutes after noon under the cover of our artillery barrage, had carried Thiepval, the north-west corner of Mouquet Farm, and the Zollern Redoubt on the eastern crest. The German pivot had gone, the pivot which they had believed impregnable. So skilful was our barrage that our men were over the German parapets and into the dug-outs before

RELIEVED CANADIAN TROOPS PASSING AMMUNITION TRAIN ON ITS WAY TO THE FIRING LINE

machine-guns could be got up to repel them. Here the prisoners were numerous, for the attack was in the nature of a surprise.

On the evening of 26th September, the Allied fortunes in the West had never looked brighter. The enemy was now on his fourth line, without the benefit of the high ground, and there was no chance of retrieving his disadvantages by observation from the air. Since 1st July the British alone had taken over twenty-six thousand prisoners, and had engaged thirty-eight German divisions, the flower of the army, of which twenty-nine had been withdrawn exhausted and broken. The enemy had been compelled to use up his reserves in repeated costly and futile counter-attacks without compelling the Allies to relax for one moment their steady and methodical pressure.

Every part of the armies of France and Britain had done gloriously, and the new divisions had shown the courage and discipline of veterans. A hundred captured documents showed that the German moral had been shaken and that the German machine was falling badly out of gear. In normal seasons at least another month of fine weather might be reasonably counted on, and in that month further blows might be struck with cumulative force. In France they spoke of a "Picardy summer"—of fair bright days at the end of autumn when the ground was dry and the air of a crystal clearness. A fortnight of such days would suffice for a crowning achievement.

The hope was destined to fail. The guns were scarcely silent after the great attack of the 26th, when the weather broke, and October was one long succession of tempestuous gales and drenching rains.

To understand the difficulties which untoward weather imposed on the Allied advance, it is necessary to grasp the nature of the fifty square miles of tortured ground which three months' fighting had given them, and over which lay the communications between their firing line and the rear. From a position like the north end of High Wood almost the whole British battle-ground on a clear day was visible to the eye. To reach the place from the old Allied front line some four miles of bad roads had to be traversed. They would have been bad roads in a moorland parish, where they suffered only the transit of the infrequent carrier's cart, for, at the best, they were mere country tracks, casually engineered, and with no solid foundation. But here they had to support such a traffic as the world had scarcely seen before.

Not the biggest mining camp or the vastest engineering undertaking had ever produced one tithe of the activity which existed behind each section of the battle line. There were places like Crewe, places like

MOVING A BIG GUN

the skirts of Birmingham, places like Alder shot or Salisbury Plain. It has often been pointed out that the immense and complex mechanism of modern armies resembles a series of pyramids which taper to a point as they near the front. Though all modern science had gone to the making of this war, at the end, in spite of every artificial aid, it became elementary, akin in many respects to the days of bows and arrows.

It was true of the whole front, but the Somme battle-ground was peculiar in this, that the area of land where the devices of civilisation broke down was far larger than elsewhere. Elsewhere it was defined more or less by the limits of the enemy's observation and fire. On the Somme it was defined by the previous three months' battle. It was not the German guns which made the trouble on the ground between the Albert-Peronne road and the British firing line. Casual bombardments troubled us little. It was the hostile elements and the unkindly nature of Mother Earth.

The country roads had been rutted out of recognition by endless transport, and, since they never had much of a bottom, the toil of the road-menders had nothing to build upon. New roads were hard to make, for the chalky soil was poor and had been so churned up by shelling and the movement of guns and troops that it had lost all cohesion. Countless shells had burst below the ground, causing everywhere subsidences and cavities. There was no stone in the countryside and little wood, so repairing materials had to be brought from a distance, which still further complicated the problem. To mend a road you must give it a rest, but there was little chance of a rest for any of those poor tortured passages. In all the district there were but two good highways, one running at right angles to our front from Albert to Bapaume, the other parallel to our old front line from Albert to Peronne.

These, to begin with, were the best type of *routes nationales*—broad, well-engineered, lined with orderly poplars. By the third month of the battle even these were showing signs of wear, and to travel on either in a motor car was a switchback journey. If the famous highroads declined, what was likely to be the condition of the country lanes which rayed around Contalmaison, Longueval, and Guillemont?

Let us take our stand at the northern angle of High Wood. It is only a spectre of a wood, a horrible place of matted tree trunks and crumbling trench lines, full of mementoes of the dead and all the dreadful debris of battle. To reach it we have walked across two miles of what once must have been breezy downland, patched with little fields of roots and grain. It is now like a waste brickfield in a decaying

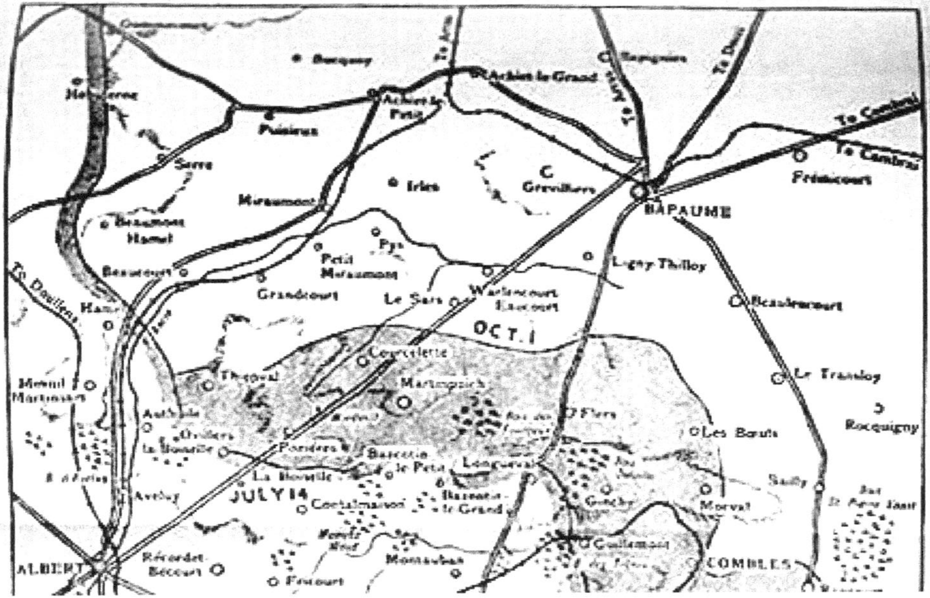
BAPAUME
To Cambrai
To Cambrai
Frémicourt
Achiet le Grand
Achiet le Petit
Puisieux
Serre
Irles
Grevillers
Miraumont
Beaumont Hamel
Petit Miraumont
Beaucourt
Grandcourt
Ligny-Thilloy
Beaulencourt
Le Sars
Warlencourt Eaucourt
To Doullens
Hamel
OCT. 1
Courcelette
Thiepval
Mesnil
Martinsart
Martinpuich
Le Transloy
Rocquigny
Les Boeufs
Ovillers
La Boisselle
Pozières
Bazentin le Petit
Longueval
JULY 14
Contalmaison
Bazentin le Grand
Aveluy
Ginchy
Morval
Sailly
Guillemont
COMBLES
Montauban
ALBERT
Bécourt
Fricourt

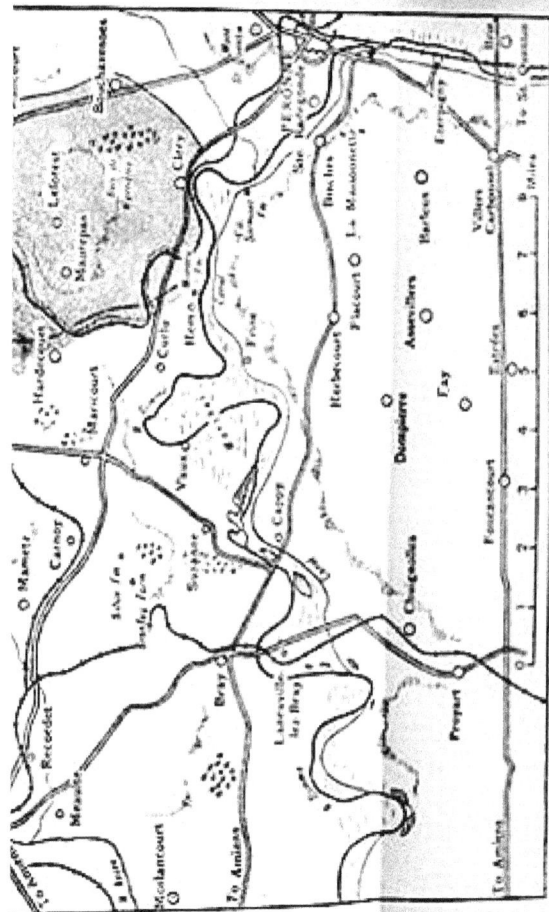

BATTLE OF THE SOMME—THE ALLIED FRONT NORTH OF THE SOMME ON OCTOBER 1ST (SHOWING THE FRONT ON JULY 14TH AND THE GROUND GAINED FROM JULY 14TH TO OCTOBER 1ST)

suburb, pock-marked with shell-holes, littered with cartridge clips, equipment, fragments of wire, and every kind of tin can. Over all the area hangs the curious, acrid, unwholesome smell of burning, an odour which will always recall to every soldier the immediate front of battle.

The air is clear, and we look from the height over a shallow trough towards the low slopes in front of the Transloy road, behind which lies the German fourth line. Our own front is some thousands of yards off, close under that hillock which is the famous Butte de Warlencourt. Far on our left is the lift of the Thiepval ridge, and nearer us, hidden by the slope, are the ruins of Martinpuich. Le Sars and Eaucourt l'Abbaye are before us, Flers a little to the right, and beyond it Gueudecourt. On our extreme right rise the slopes of Sailly-Saillisel—one can see the shattered trees lining the Bapaume-Peronne road—and, hidden by the fall of the ground, are Lesboeufs and Morval. Behind us are things like scarred patches on the hillsides. They are the remains of the Bazentin woods and the ominous wood of Delville. The whole confines of the British battle-ground lie open to the eye from the Thiepval ridge in the north to the downs which ring the site of Combles.

Look west, and beyond the dreary country we have crossed rise green downs set with woods untouched by shell—the normal, pleasant land of Picardy. Look east, beyond our front line and the smoke puffs, across the Warlencourt and Gueudecourt ridges, and on the skyline there also appear unbroken woods, and here and there a church spire and the smoke of villages. The German retirement in September had been rapid, and we have reached the fringes of a land as yet little scarred by combat. We are looking at the boundaries of the battlefield. We have pushed the enemy right up to the edge of habitable and undevastated country, but we pay for our success in having behind us a strip of sheer desolation.

There were now two No Man's Lands. One was between the front lines; the other lay between the old enemy front and the front we had won. The second was the bigger problem, for across it must be brought the supplies of a great army. This was a war of motor transport, and we were doing today what the Early Victorians pronounced impossible—running the equivalent of steam engines not on prepared tracks, but on highroads, running them day and night in endless relays. And these highroads were not the decent macadamised ways of England, but roads which would be despised in Sutherland or Connaught.

The problem was hard enough in fine weather; but let the rain come and soak the churned-up soil and the whole land became a morass. There was no *pavé*, as in Flanders, to make a firm causeway. Every road became a water-course, and in the hollows the mud was as deep as a man's thighs. An army must be fed, troops must be relieved, guns must be supplied, and so there could be no slackening of the traffic. Off the roads the ground was a squelching bog, dug-outs crumbled in, and communication trenches ceased to be. In areas like Ypres and Festubert, where the soil was naturally water-logged, the conditions were worse, but at Ypres and Festubert we had not six miles of sponge, varied by mud torrents, across which all transport must pass.

Weather is a vital condition of success in operations where great armies are concerned, for men and guns cannot fight on air. In modern war it is more urgent than ever, since aerial reconnaissance plays so great a part, and Napoleon's "fifth element," mud, grows in importance with the complexity of the fighting machine. Again, in semi-static trench warfare, where the same area remains for long the battlefield, the condition of the ground is the first fact to be reckoned with. Once we grasp this, the difficulty of the October campaign, waged in almost continuous rain, will be apparent. But no words can convey an adequate impression of the Somme area after a week's downpour. Its discomforts had to be endured to be understood.

The topography of the immediate battle-ground demands a note from the point of view of its tactical peculiarities. The British line at the end of September ran from the Schwaben Redoubt, 1,000 yards north of Thiepval, along the ridge to a point north-east of Courcelette; then just in front of Martinpuich, Flers, Gueudecourt, and Lesboeufs to the junction with the French. Morval was now part of the French area. From Thiepval to the north-east of Courcelette the line was for the most part on the crest of the ridge; it then bent southward and followed generally the foot of the eastern slopes. But a special topographical feature complicated the position.

Before our front a shallow depression ran north-west from north of Sailly-Saillisel to about 2,000 yards south of Bapaume, where it turned westward and joined the glen of the Ancre at Miraumont. From the main Thiepval-Morval ridge a series of long spurs descended into this valley, of which two were of special importance. One was the hammer-headed spur immediately west of Flers, at the western end of which stood the tumulus called the Butte de Warlencourt.

The other was a spur which, lying across the main trend of the ground, ran north from Morval to Thilloy, passing 1,000 yards to the

113

east of Gueudecourt. Behind these spurs lay the German fourth position. It was in the main a position on reverse slopes, and so screened from immediate observation, though our command of the higher ground gave us a view of its hinterland. Our own possession of the heights, great though its advantages were, had certain drawbacks, for it meant that our communications had to make the descent of the reverse slopes and were thus exposed to some extent to the enemy's observation and long-range fire.

The next advance of the British Army had therefore two distinct objectives. The first—the task of the Fourth Army—was to carry the two spurs and so get within assaulting distance of the German fourth line. Even if the grand assault should be postponed, the possession of the spurs would greatly relieve our situation, by giving us cover for our advanced gun positions and a certain shelter for the bringing up of supplies. It should be remembered that the spurs were not part of the German main front. They were held by the enemy as intermediate positions, and very strongly held—every advantage being taken of sunken roads, buildings, and the undulating nature of the country. They represented for the fourth German line what Contalmaison had represented for the second; till they were carried no general assault on the main front could be undertaken. The second task—that of the Fifth Army—was to master the whole of the high ground on the Thiepval ridge, so as to get direct observation into the Ancre glen and over the uplands north and northeast of it.

The expected fine weather of October did not come. On the contrary, the month provided a record in wet, spells of drenching rain being varied by dull, misty days, so that the sodden land had no chance of drying. The carrying of the spurs—meant as a preliminary step to a general attack—proved an operation so full of difficulties that it occupied all our efforts during the month, and with it all was not completed. The story of these weeks is one of minor operations, local actions with strictly limited objectives undertaken by only a few battalions. In the face of every conceivable difficulty, we moved gradually up the intervening slopes.

At first there was a certain briskness in our movement. From Flers north-westward, in front of Eaucourt l'Abbaye and Le Sars, ran a very strong trench system, which we called the Flers line, and which was virtually a switch connecting the old German third line with the intermediate positions in front of the spurs. The capture of Flers gave us the south-eastern part of the line, and the last days of September

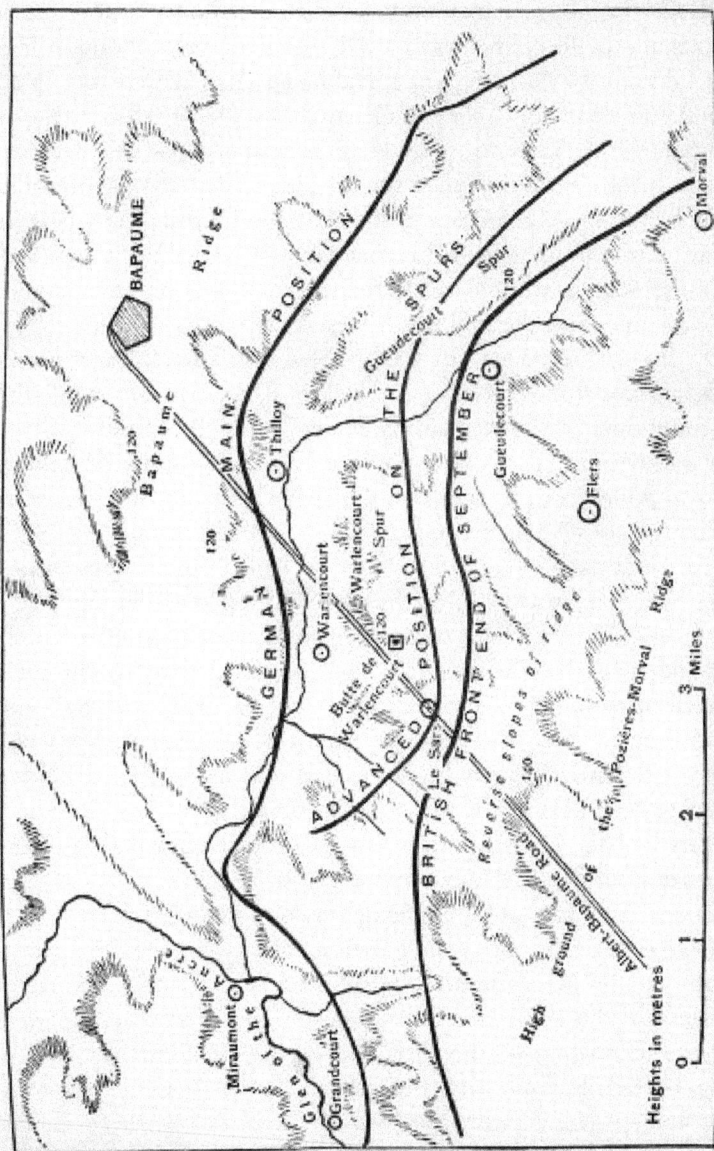

BATTLE OF THE SOMME—THE GUEUDECOURT AND WARLENCOURT SPURS

and the first of October were occupied in winning the remainder of it. On 29th September a single company of a Northumbrian division carried the farm of Destremont, some 400 yards south-west of Le Sars and just north of the Albert-Bapaume road.

On the afternoon of 1st October, we advanced on a front of 3,000 yards, taking the Flers line north of Destremont, while a London Territorial division—the same which had taken High Wood—occupied the buildings of the old abbey of Eaucourt, less than a mile south-east of Le Sars village. Here for several days remnants of the 6th Bavarian Division made a stout resistance. On the morning of 2nd October, the enemy had regained a footing in the abbey, and during the whole of the next day and night the battle fluctuated. It was not till the morning of the 4th that we finally cleared the place, and on 6th October the Londoners won the mill north-west of it.

On the afternoon of 7th October—a day of cloud and strong winds, but free from rain—we attacked on a broader front, while the French on our right moved against the key position of Sailly-Saillisel. After a heavy struggle a division of the New Army captured Le Sars and won positions to the east and west of it, while our line was considerably advanced between Gueudecourt and Lesboeufs.

From that date for a month on we struggled up the slopes, gaining ground, but never winning the crests. The enemy now followed a new practice. He had his machine-guns well back in prepared positions and caught our attack with their long-range fire. To chronicle in detail those indeterminate actions would be a laborious task, and would demand for its elucidation a map on the largest scale. We wrestled for odd lengths of fantastically named trenches which were often three feet deep in water. It was no light job to get out over the slimy parapets, and the bringing up of supplies and the evacuation of the wounded placed a terrible burden on our strength.

Under conditions of such grievous discomfort an attack on a comprehensive scale was out of the question, the more when we remember the condition of the area behind our lines. At one moment it seemed as if the Butte had been won. On 5th November we were over it and holding positions on the eastern side, but that night a counter-attack by fresh troops of the 4th Guard Division—who had just come up—forced us to fall back. This was the one successful enemy counter-stroke in this stage of the battle. For the most part they were too weak, if delivered promptly; and when they came later in strength they were broken up by our guns.

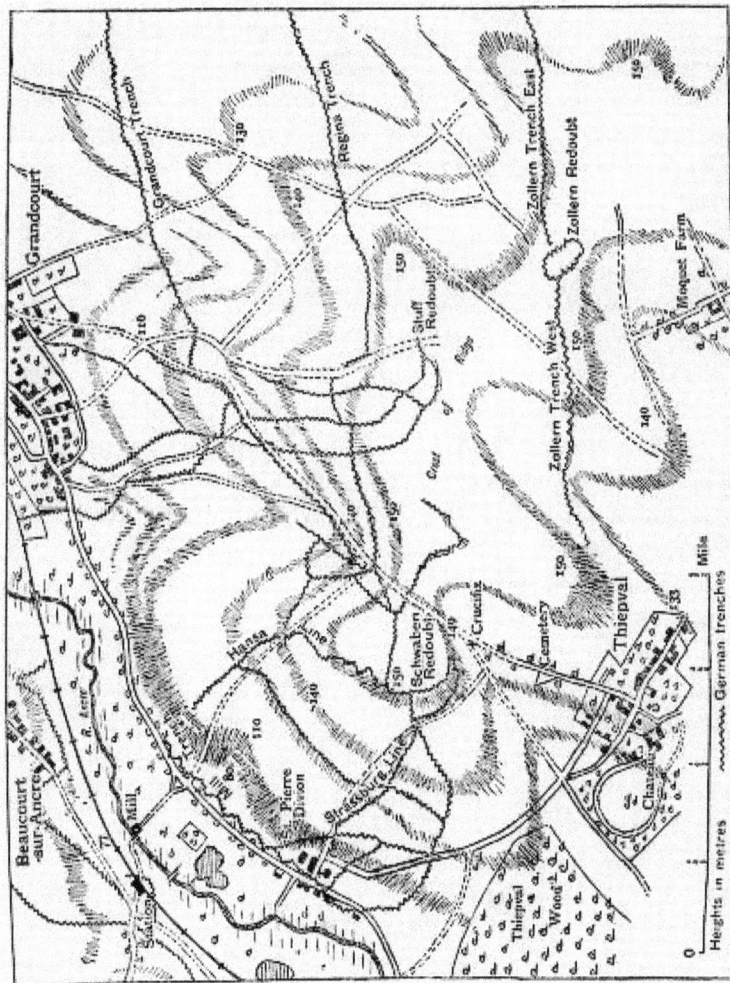

BATTLE OF THE SOMME—THE THIEPVAL RIDGE

Heights in metres

0         ½ Mile

~~~~~ German Trenches

Grandcourt

Beaucourt-sur-Ancre

Station

Mill

R. Ancre

Grandcourt Trench

Regina Trench

Zollern Trench East

Zollern Redoubt

Zollern Trench West

Stuff Redoubt

Mouquet Farm

Crest

Hansa Line

Strassburg Line

Schwaben Redoubt

Crucifix

Cemetery

Thiepval

Château

Pierre Divon

Thiepval Wood

130

110

120

150

100

150

140

130

140

150

140

150

150

150

150

130

110

140

33

The struggle of these days deserves to rank high in the records of British hardihood. The fighting had not the swift pace and the brilliant successes of the September battles. Our men had to fight for minor objectives, and such a task lacks the impetus and exhilaration of a great combined assault. On many occasions the battle resolved itself into isolated struggles, a handful of men in a mud-hole holding out and consolidating their ground till their post was linked up with our main front. Rain, cold, slow reliefs, the absence of hot food, and sometimes of any food at all, made these episodes a severe test of endurance and devotion. During this period the enemy, amazed at his good fortune, inasmuch as the weather had crippled our advance, fell into a flamboyant mood and represented the result as a triumph of the fighting quality of his own troops.

From day to day, he announced a series of desperate British assaults invariably repulsed with heavy losses. He spoke of British corps and divisions advancing in massed formation, when, at the most, it had been an affair of a few battalions. Often, he announced an attack on a day and in a locality where nothing whatever had happened. It is worth remembering that, except for the highly successful action of 21st October, which we shall presently record, there was no British attack during the month on anything like a large scale, and that the various minor actions, so far from having cost us high, were among the most economical of the campaign.

Our second task, in which we brilliantly succeeded, was to master completely the Thiepval ridge. By the end of September, the strong redoubts northeast of the village—called Stuff and Zollern—were in our hands, and on the 28th of that month we had carried all Schwaben Redoubt except the north-west corner. It was Schwaben Redoubt to which the heroic advance of the Ulster Division had penetrated on the first day of the battle; but next day the advanced posts had been drawn in, and three months had elapsed before we again entered it.

It was now a very different place from 1st July. Our guns had pounded it out of recognition; but it remained—from its situation—the pivot of the whole German line on the heights. Thence the trenches called Stuff and Regina ran east for some 5,000 yards to a point north-east of Courcelette. These trenches, representing many of the dominating points of the ridge south of the Ancre, were defended by the enemy with the most admirable tenacity.

Between 30th September and 20th October, while we were battling for the last corner of the Schwaben, he delivered not less than

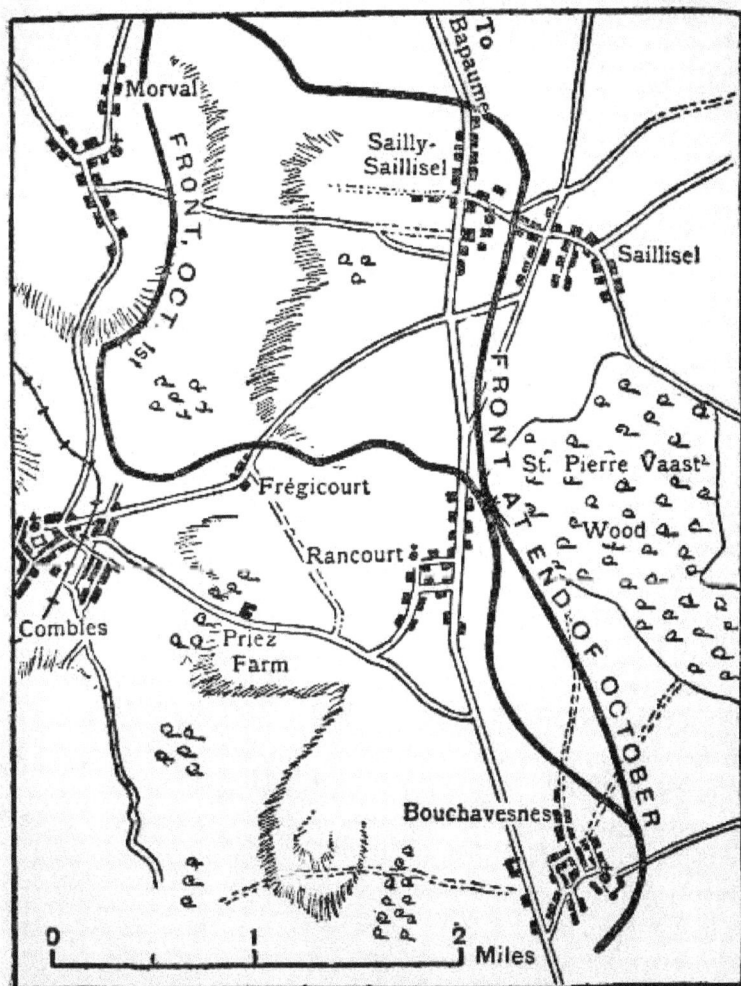

BATTLE OF THE SOMME.—THE FRENCH ADVANCE DURING OCTOBER NORTH OF THE SOMME.

eleven counter-attacks against our front in that neighbourhood, counter-attacks which in every case were repulsed with heavy losses. His front was held by the 26th Reserve Division and by Marines of the Naval Division, who had been brought down from the Yser, and who gave a better account of themselves than their previous record had led us to expect. A captured German regimental order, dated 20th October, emphasised the necessity of regaining the Schwaben Redoubt.

Men are to be informed by their immediate superiors that this attack is not merely a matter of retaking a trench because it was formerly in German possession, but that the recapture of an extremely important point is involved. If the enemy remains on the ridge, he can blow our artillery in the Ancre valley to pieces, and the protection of the infantry will then be destroyed.

From 20th October to 23rd there came a short spell of fine weather. There was frost at night, a strong easterly wind dried the ground, and the air conditions were perfect for observation. The enemy was quick to take advantage of the change, and early on the morning of Saturday, 21st October, delivered that attack upon the Schwaben Redoubt for which the order quoted above was a preparation.

The attack was made in strength, and at all points but two were repulsed by our fire before reaching our lines. At two points the Germans entered our trenches, but were promptly driven out, leaving many dead in front of our positions, and five officers and seventy-nine other ranks prisoners in our hands.

This counter-stroke came opportunely for us, for it enabled us to catch the enemy on the rebound. We struck shortly after noon, attacking against the whole length of the Regina trench, with troops of the New Army on our left and centre and the Canadians on our right. The attack was completely successful, for the enemy, disorganised by his failure of the morning, was in no condition for prolonged resistance. We attained all our objectives, taking the whole of Stuff and Regina trenches, pushing out advanced posts well to the north and north-east of Schwaben Redoubt, and establishing our position on the crown of the ridge between the Upper Ancre and Courcelette. In the course of the day, we took nearly 1,100 prisoners at the expense of less than 1,200 casualties, many of which were extremely slight. The whole course of the battle showed no more workmanlike performance.

There still remained one small section of the ridge where our position was unsatisfactory. This was at the extreme eastern end of Regina trench, just west of the Bapaume road. Its capture was achieved on the night of 10th November, when we carried it on a front of 1,000 yards. This rounded off our gains and allowed us to dominate the upper valley of the Ancre and the uplands beyond it behind the unbroken German first line from Beaumont Hamel to Serre.

Meantime, during the month, the French Armies on our right had pressed forward. At the end of September, they had penetrated into St. Pierre Vaast Wood, whose labyrinthine depths extended east of Rancourt and south of Saillisel. The British gains of 26th September filled the whole French nation with enthusiasm, and General Joffre and Sir Douglas Haig exchanged the warmest greetings. The immediate object of the forces under Foch was to cooperate with the British advance by taking the height of Sailly-Saillisel, and so to work round Mont St. Quentin, the main defence of Peronne on the north.

On 4th October they carried the German intermediate line between Morval and St. Pierre Vaast Wood, and on 8th October—in a splendid movement—they swept up the Sailly-Saillisel slopes and won the Bapaume-Peronne road to a point 200 yards from its northern entry into the village. On 10th October Micheler's Tenth Army was in action on a front of three miles, and carried the western outskirts of Ablaincourt and the greater part of the wood north-west of Chaulnes, taking nearly 1,300 prisoners. On the 15th Fayolle pushed east of Bouchavesnes, and on the same day, south of the Somme, Micheler, after beating off a counter-attack, carried a mile and a quarter of the German front west of Belloy, and advanced well to the north-east of Ablaincourt, taking some 1,000 prisoners. This brought the French nearer to the ridge of Villers-Carbonnel, behind which the German batteries played the same part for the southern defence of Peronne as Mont St. Quentin did for the northern.

Next day Sailly-Saillisel was entered and occupied as far as the cross-roads, the Saillisel section of the village on the road running eastwards being still in German hands. For the next few days, the enemy delivered violent counter-attacks from both north and east, using liquid fire, but they failed to oust the garrison, and that part of the village held by the Germans was mercilessly pounded by the French guns. On the 21st newly arrived 2nd Bavarian Division made a desperate attack from the southern border of Saillisel and the ridge northeast of St. Pierre Vaast Wood, but failed with many losses. There were other heavy and fruitless counter-strokes south of the Somme in the regions of Biaches and Chaulnes. The month closed with the

121

POINTING A HEAVY GUN

French holding Sailly but not Saillisel; holding the western skirts of St. Pierre Vaast Wood, and south of the river outflanking Ablaincourt and Chaulnes.

The record of the month, though short of expectations, was far from mediocre; and, considering the difficulties of weather, was not less creditable than that of September. The Allies at one point had broken into the German fourth position, while at others they had won positions of assault against it, and the southward extension of the battle-ground had been greatly deepened. They had added another 10,000 prisoners to their roll, bringing the total from 1st July to 1,469 officers and 71,532 other ranks, while they had also taken 173 field guns, 130 heavy pieces, 215 trench mortars, and 988 machine-guns. They had engaged ninety enemy divisions, of which twenty-six had been taken out, refitted, and sent back again—making a total of 116 brought into action. On 1st November the enemy was holding his front with twenty-one divisions, so that ninety-five had been used up and withdrawn.

Any calculation of enemy losses during the actual progress of operations must be a very rough estimate, but it may be taken for granted that no German division was taken out of the line till it had lost at least 5,000 men. This gives a minimum figure for enemy losses during the four months' battle of close on half a million, and it seems certain that the real figure was at least 25 *per cent,* greater. It must further be noted that, according to the German published returns, 41 *per cent,* of their casualties were irreplaceable—dead, prisoners, or so badly wounded as to be useless for the remainder of the war—a proportion greatly in excess of that which obtained among the Allies.

During the month of October, the British casualties were little beyond those of a normal month of trench warfare. The study of captured documents cast an interesting light upon the condition of the enemy under the pressure of our attacks. Letters of individual soldiers and the reports of commanding officers alike showed that the strain had been very great. There were constant appeals to troops to hold some point as vital to the whole position, and these points invariably fell into our hands. There were endless complaints of the ruin wrought by our artillery and of the ceaseless activity of our aircraft, and there were many unwilling tributes to the fighting quality of the Allied soldiers.

But though indications of weakened enemy morale and failure in enemy organisation were frequent, he was still a most formidable

HEAVY GUN IN ACTION

antagonist. He had accumulated his best troops and batteries on the Somme front, and was fighting with the stubborn resolution of those who knew that they were facing the final peril, and that they alone stood between their country and defeat.

In the various actions the work of the Allied artillery was extraordinarily efficient. Their barrages brilliantly covered the advance of the infantry; they searched out and silenced enemy batteries; they destroyed great lengths of enemy trenches and countless enemy strongholds; and they kept up a continuous fire behind the enemy's front, interfering with the movement of troops and supplies, and giving him no peace for eight or ten miles behind his line. The "tanks," though only occasionally used, had some remarkable achievements to their credit. On a certain day one got behind the enemy's front, and by itself compelled the surrender of a whole battalion, including the battalion commander. Much credit was due also to the transport service, which faithfully performed its duties under the most trying conditions.

The weather was bad for all, but perhaps it was worst for our aircraft. The strong south-westerly gales greatly increased the complexity of their task, since our machines were drifted far behind the enemy's front and compelled to return against a head-wind, which made their progress slow and thereby exposed them to fire, and, in the case of a damaged engine, forbade a glide into safety. Yet, in spite of adverse conditions, they showed in the highest degree the spirit of the offensive. They patrolled regularly far behind the enemy lines, and fought many battles in the air with hostile machines, and many with enemy troops on the ground. They did much valuable reconnaissance, and repeatedly attacked with success enemy lines of communication, ammunition dumps, billets, and depots.

Toward the latter part of October, the German machines were more in evidence, but we dealt satisfactorily with this increased activity. As an instance of the audacity of our aviators we may quote the case of one pilot who, encountering a formation of ten hostile machines, attacked them single-handed and dispersed them far behind their own front.

We inflicted many losses on the foe, but we did not go scatheless ourselves. The curt announcement in the *communiqués*—"One of our machines has not returned"—covered many a tale of bravery and misfortune. About half the missing came down in enemy territory and were made prisoners; the others perished in battle in the air, shot by machine or anti-aircraft gun, or dashed to earth by a crippled air-

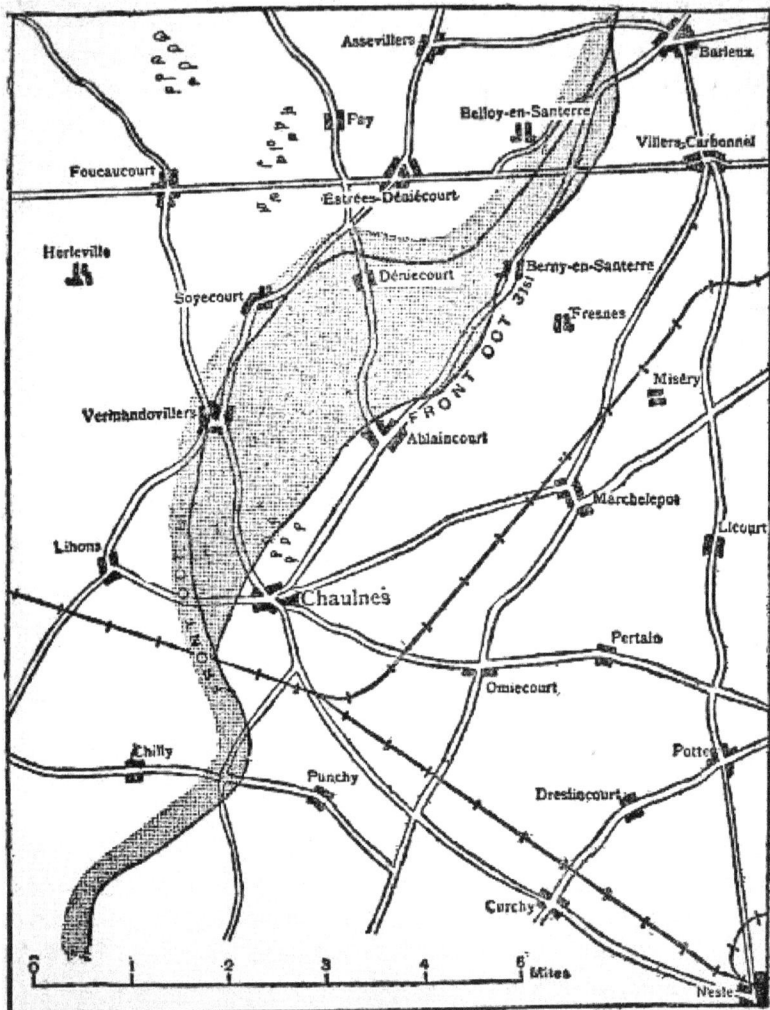

Asservillers
Barleux
Fay
Belloy-en-Santerre
Villers-Carbonnel
Foucaucourt
Estrées-Déniécourt
Herleville
Berny-en-Santerre
Déniécourt
Soyecourt
Fresnes
Misery
Verinandovillers
Ablaincourt
Marchelepot
Lihons
Licourt
Chaulnes
Pertain
Omiecourt
Chilly
Pottes
Punchy
Dreslincourt
Curchy
Neste

FRONT OCT 31st

O    1    2    3    4    5  Miles

BATTLE OF THE SOMME.—THE FRENCH ADVANCE DURING OCTOBER SOUTH
OF THE SOMME (SHOWING THE FRONT OF THE TENTH ARMY ON OCT.
1ST, AND THE GROUND GAINED DURING THE MONTH).

plane. In a flight over the German lines on 4th November there died one of the most gallant figures of our day, conspicuous even in the universal heroism of his service. Lord Lucas, whom Oxford of twenty years ago knew as "Bron Herbert," had joined the Flying Corps at the age of forty. He had lost a leg in the South African War; he had had a distinguished political career, culminating in a seat in the Cabinet as President of the Board of Agriculture; he had great possessions and a thousand ties to ease; if ever man might have found his reasonable duty in a less perilous sphere it was he.

But after the formation of the Coalition Government in May 1915, he went straight into training for his pilot's certificate, and soon proved himself an exceptionally bold and skilful aviator. He did good work in Egypt, whence he returned in the spring of 1916, and after a few months spent in instructing recruits at home he came out to France in the early autumn. He was one who retained in all his many activities the adventurous zest and the strange endearing simplicity of a boy. With his genius for happiness the world in which he dwelt could never be a common place. In the air he found the pure exultant joy of living that he had always sought, and he passed out of life like some hero of romance, with his ardour undimmed and his dream untarnished.

★★★★★★★★★★

"When the Greeks made their fine saying that those whom the gods love die young, I cannot help believing they had this sort of death in their eye. For surely, at whatever age it overtakes the man, this is to die young. Death has not been suffered to take so much as an illusion from his heart. In the hot-fit of life, a tiptoe on the highest point of being, he passes at a bound on to the other side. The noise of the mallet and chisel is scarcely quenched, the trumpets are hardly done blowing, when, trailing with him clouds of glory, this happy-starred, full-blooded spirit shoots into the spiritual land."—R. L. Stevenson, *Æs Triplex*.

★★★★★★★★★★

www.ingramcontent.com/pod-product-compliance
Lightning Source LLC
Chambersburg PA
CBHW031856090426
42741CB00005B/522